∽ **Presentation Page** ∾

Presented by

_____

Presented to

_____

❧ 123 Incredible Events ☙ That Shook the World & Transformed the Church

For information contact Belle Rive Publishers, 115 Penn Warren Drive, Suite 300, Box 321, Brentwood, Tennessee 37027.

Scripture quotations are from The Holy Bible, New Living Translation copyright © 1996 by Tyndale Charitable Trust. Used by permission of Tyndale House Publishers.

Certain text has been adapted from the public domain writings of Henry K. Rowe and Charles S. Nutter.

Printed in the United States of America.

ISBN # 0-9753409-4-8

First Printing, September 2004

1 2 3 4 5 6 7 8 9 — 08 07 06 05 04

The Church is like a great ship pounded by the waves . . . Our job is not to abandon the ship but to keep it on its course.
St. Boniface

Number 1: The first Christian martyr

In the period immediately after Christ's death and resurrection, Christians were viewed as one of many local religions and were left alone. Only on occasion were believers silenced when their preaching threatened a public disturbance. But as time passed and the number of Christians multiplied a clash with the old order occurred. This first happened when Stephen was arrested and brought before the Sanhedrin in Jerusalem for preaching among the Hellenists that the sacrificial death of Jesus was more important than the letter of the Jewish law. To question the validity of the law was considered blasphemy. He was condemned and stoned to death.

Impact: The death of Stephen launched the first active persecution of believers. The arrest and execution of Christians became so frequent that they fled from the city for safety. Throughout Judea and Samaria they scattered, carrying with them the Gospel of Jesus.

Number 2: The conversion of Paul

The growth of Christianity depended largely on its leadership. The Galilean leaders were an uneducated group who had never been outside of Palestine. Paul was well suited for the role of leader and organizer. Jewish by birth and training, he was reared in a Greek city and he inherited Roman citizenship. He was also a Pharisee and had been a persecutor of Christians at Damascus. Though at first distrusted after his dramatic conversion by those he had opposed, his abilities brought him to the forefront and after several years he was commissioned as a missionary by a conference of several members of the Church at Antioch.

Impact: Paul's tireless efforts to spread the Gospel, his skills as a teacher, his compassion, and his inspired writings were key reasons why the early church survived and thrived.

Number 3: The Jerusalem Council

After his first missionary trip in about 47 Paul came to realize the importance of bringing the Gospel message to Gentiles as well as Jews. He decided it was wise to first get the endorsement of the Jerusalem community of Christians. He could have gone his own way for the Jerusalem Church had no jurisdiction over other Christians, but it enjoyed a prestige greater than other groups and Paul felt it was best to preserve harmony. He went to Jerusalem after his return from Asia Minor, told his story of Gentile conversions to the leaders there, and urged their support. The Jerusalem believers were naturally more conservative than Paul, but after extended discussion a compromise was reached. Later in a public conference the Jerusalem Christians agreed that Paul should be free to preach to the Gentiles, and that nothing more should be required of the converts than certain abstinences. It was decided, though, that Palestinian Christians must keep the rules of Jewish law.

Impact: This conference, held in about the year 50, not only set the course for the future of missionary outreach it also signaled Paul's supremacy over Peter in the leadership of the early church.

Number 4: The threat of Gnosticism

The early Christians believed in Jesus and accepted him for what he claimed to be, Messiah and Lord. The Gnostics taught a form of Platonic dualism between the spiritual and the material, and said that Christ could not have lived an actual human life and have also been God. He was one of many spirits, they said, and did not really acquire human form, though he seemed to. Such assertions were obviously heretical and were the first instance where truth was challenged by false teaching.

Impact: The competition with Gnosticism compelled the early Christians to define and defend their faith, and supplied certain of the technical terms of later theology. With the aid of apologists and teachers the Church worked itself free from Gnosticism. Several of the eminent champions of orthodoxy drew up simple statements of belief as rules of faith. One of the first to do this was Ignatius of Antioch who wrote that Jesus was "truly born, ate and drank, truly suffered persecution under Pontius Pilate, was truly crucified and died, who was also truly raised from the dead, his Father raising him up." Such rules of faith as this became standards in the local churches, and later they were elaborated into creeds, like the Apostles' Creed.

Number 5: The establishment of the Gospels
Christians did not depend at first on written sources for
their faith. They accepted the Old Testament as sacred,
but the New Testament was created and collected
gradually. For four or five decades after the death of Jesus
the story of his life and message was transmitted orally.
The earliest written Gospel was Mark, which told the basic
details of the life of Jesus. A few years later came the
Gospel of Matthew, whose story is fuller. Because of the
high regard in which it was held, it was placed as the first
of the Gospels at the very beginning of the New Testament
collection. These Gospels were supplemented by the Greek
account of Luke. Here Gentile Christians had a sketch of
the events and the teachings of Jesus. The Gospel according
to John interpreted the mind and character of Jesus in
language familiar to the religious thinkers of the Hellenistic
age.
Impact: As soon as the first written Gospels were available
they were read in the churches. Every church had its own
collection of manuscript rolls, which were highly prized.

Number 6: The establishment of the Epistles
Paul wrote letters during his travels to give counsel or
comfort when he was unable to visit the churches he had
organized. Some of these were composed principally of
practical admonitions and reminders of his presence with
them. Others contained discussions of religious convictions
and cautions against false ideas. The earliest of Paul's
epistles was very likely the letter to the Galatians. He had

made his first missionary journey here after he had been commissioned at Antioch. He was disturbed by the report that Judaizers had been at work trying to make the Gentile Christians believe that they must obey Jewish laws, and he reminded them forcibly that he had given them a gospel of liberty and showed the grounds of their freedom. Perhaps his greatest letter was sent in anticipation of a visit to Rome. In Romans he explains the great doctrines of Christianity including justification, sanctification, and the freedom of the Gospel. Paul's letters reveal that he was an affectionate pastor, a great and confident leader, and a man fully inspired by God.

Impact: Paul's letters established much of the framework upon which Christian doctrine is built.

Number 7: The establishment of the Canon

Although the letters of Paul were written to special groups of Christians they were welcomed and read by churches everywhere. Paul's letters and the Gospels soon were deemed worthy of a place in a new collection of sacred writings. With them were other documents that received the ultimate approval of the Christian people including the Acts of the Apostles, written by Luke to explain the beginnings of the church; a number of brief letters from key Christian leaders; the anonymous letter to the Hebrews; and the Apocalypse written by the Apostle John. Writings like Acts and the letters to Timothy and Titus received immediate acceptance, but less known documents such as the general epistles were slower to receive recognition.

Some of them were esteemed in the East and others in the West, as shown by two documentary evidences, one the Syriac Bible of the East, an early version, and the other the Muratorian Fragment, a list discovered in the eighteenth century. In the fourth century official sanction was given by synods in North Africa.

Impact: The Festal Letter of Athanasius in 367 contains the names of twenty-six books of the New Testament, the same as now. The establishment of the canon set the foundation upon which the Church was built.

Number 8: The writings of the Apostolic Fathers

Aside from the New Testament few important Christian writings existed before the middle of the second century. But practical problems of Christian life or church administration prompted several writers to express their opinions. They are called the Apostolic Fathers. The earliest of these writers was Clement of Rome, who in about the year 96 wrote to the Christians at Corinth a letter of friendly counsel. He blamed them for their dissension and their rebellion against their church leaders. Ignatius, head of the church at Antioch, wrote several letters to Christian churches as he traveled to Rome in 115 where he was martyred. In these letters he emphasized the importance of the bishop's office. Polycarp, an aged bishop of the church at Smyrna, who also suffered death for his faith in the same period, wrote an affectionate letter to the church at Philippi. None of these letters are statements of doctrine or systematic discussions of organization or worship, but they deal with matters that were important to Christian leaders of the day. A fourth letter of the same period bears the name of Barnabas, though there is no evidence that the companion of Paul wrote it. The *Didache*, or *Teaching of the Twelve Apostles*, originated in Syria or Egypt and was influential among the churches of the Near East. While the first part of the *Didache* was spiritually edifying, the second part dealt with such details as church government, the role of ministers, and the Second Coming of Christ. A sixth document, which dates from the end of the Apostolic Age, is the *Shepherd of Hermas*, which was so highly esteemed that it was read frequently at services of worship. It is an allegory that tells of a shepherd who brings a message of repentance to Christians.

Impact: These writings encouraged the early Christians and give scholars today information about a period of early Christian history that is otherwise relatively obscure.

Number 9: The writings of the Apologists

A third group of writers were intellectuals who provided a systematic defense of Christianity. Known as Apologists, they were men who had been educated in classical culture and were recognized leaders in the churches. They denied the charges made against the Christians, addressed the emperor or the senate in a plea for justice, contended against Gnosticism and paganism, and tried to preserve traditional teachings that had come down from the Apostolic Age. Athenagoras used philosophy to defend Christianity. Aristides set forth Christianity as the highest development of ancient religion. Latin Apologists in the third century aggressively attacked paganism with strong confidence in the coming victory of their faith. Minucius Felix, a Roman lawyer, was perhaps the first apologist to use the Latin language in defining Christianity. Justin Martyr is the best-known Apologist. He was of heathen parentage and was trained in Greek philosophy in the schools of Asia Minor. In his *Apology* he defended Christianity and explained Christian worship. In his *Dialogue* he told of his own long search for truth from Stoicism to Platonism and eventually to Christianity.

Impact: The result of the writings of the apologists was to dignify Christianity and give it a place as a reasoned system of thought, not merely as a passing spiritual fad.

Number 10: The writings of the Church Fathers

Certain leaders of great prominence in the second century are called distinctively Church Fathers. Irenæus, the Bishop of Lyons in Gaul, was a theologian who centered his writings on the relationship of the Son to the Father. He also wrote about salvation, the importance of baptism, and the need to follow apostolic tradition. Tertullian of Carthage was educated for the law and he used legal language in his theological definitions. He introduced certain words into the theological vocabulary, like "substance" and "merit." He brought the word "Trinity" into theological use, and made the personality of the Holy Spirit distinct. He distinguished the two natures in Christ in a way that foreshadowed the later thinking of the Greek Fathers.

Impact: The Church Fathers anticipated Augustine by two centuries in their formulation of the doctrine of original sin and in their acceptance of the principle of divine grace.

Number 11: The early Christian schools

If Christian apologists were to hold their own against the various kinds of opposition they met, and new Christian leaders were to understand Christianity and not be led astray, schools were necessary. The earliest disciples had sat at the feet of Jesus. Christians of the second and third generations instructed the young in apostolic tradition and in the Bible. But late in the second century the establishment of catechetical schools was needed to supplement this instruction. Alexandria especially enjoyed such a great reputation as an educational center that it was the logical place for a Christian school. Connected with the Christian school in Alexandria were two young men who became successively the headmasters and who put their mark on the mind of the Eastern Church. These teachers were Clement and Origen. Clement never swerved from his conviction that Christ was the source and center of all knowledge. He believed that God dwelt in humanity and gave humanity its worth. Like the Greek Fathers he trusted the power of the human will to set a person's feet along the right path. Origen, who was highly educated, probed deeper into the mysteries of Christianity than others before him. He remained for many years at the head of the school, though he traveled widely in search of manuscripts and was in demand for spiritual counsel. He compiled the

Hexapla, using six biblical texts in parallel columns for purposes of comparison and was a great exegetical scholar.
Impact: The schools, especially the one in Alexandria, preserved early writings and produced important scholars who impacted the church for centuries.

Number 12: Early persecutions

Early Christians were charged by pagans with being guilty of sedition and of conducting immoral gatherings in secret. The Emperor Nero burned Christians on certain occasions to light his palace gardens. Domitian had persecuted believers because he was suspicious of their religious associations and their possible political ambitions. In Trajan's time, about 100, Christians could be tried at will and punished with death if they were found guilty. This policy of judicial procedure was followed for 150 years. Prominent leaders at various times were victims of intolerance, including Ignatius, Polycarp, and Justin. Outbreaks of active persecution were severe at times in certain provinces, notably North Africa. After an outbreak of hostility in the reign of Septimius Severus Christians enjoyed a long period of immunity. This was favorable for the rapid growth of the church. Alarmed at this growth the Emperor Decius inaugurated a renewed policy of suppression during his short reign; which was followed by Valerian, who adopted the same policy. Large numbers of persons were arrested and tortured, and many of them were put to death. Those who endured the persecution faithfully were spoken of as "confessors" and were honored by their fellow Christians. Again a period of toleration ensued for forty years, followed by the worst of all the persecutions, which raged for years.

Impact: The faithfulness of Christian martyrs had a great influence on those who witnessed their courage and, as a result, countless men and women converted to the faith.

Number 13: Christianity is made legal

When Diocletian abdicated and rival Cæsars fought one another for the imperial throne, Constantine emerged a victor. He was wise enough to see that Christianity was too strong to be uprooted, and that the Christians must be given official sanction. Christians were more representative of all classes and were more respected than a century earlier. In the year 311 it was decreed "that liberty of worship shall not be denied to any, but that the mind and will of every individual shall be free to manage divine affairs according to his own choice and that every person who cherishes the desire to observe the Christian religion shall freely and unconditionally proceed to observe the same without hindrance." The recognition of Christianity by Constantine was one of the principal landmarks in the history of the Christian people. At last after three hundred years of uncertainty and peril they could feel secure. Without fear Christians could build their churches, meet for discussion of church interests, and read freely the Scriptures the authorities had tried to destroy.

Impact: By making Christianity a legal religion, Constantine opened the door for one of the greatest periods of growth in the history of the church.

Number 14: The Donatist controversy

During the final and most severe persecution of the Christians a special attempt was made to destroy their sacred books. Hundreds of Christians in North Africa surrendered copies of manuscripts they possessed in order to save themselves. Even the clergy in some cases were guilty of being "traditors," as such persons were called. Those who had proved faithful would not have fellowship with such persons, much less accept their leadership. The result was a separatist organization formed in 315 by Donatus, after whom they were called Donatists. Many Donatist churches were created in North Africa and elsewhere, in spite of Catholic and imperial opposition. Aside from their desire for severity of church discipline, the Donatists were notable for their conviction that the clergy must be men of high character or else their work was ineffective. It was a Donatist practice, therefore, to rebaptize persons who joined them from a church whose clergy were not highly esteemed. The question of rebaptism occasioned some controversy among the orthodox. True to the Catholic principle that the act of baptism and not the administrator was the important matter, Rome took the position that no rebaptism was necessary.

Impact: Synods were held at Carthage at which an anti-Roman position was ratified. But the Roman influence was the stronger, and in the end Augustine fixed the position of the Catholic Church by affirming that once a person was baptized they could be readmitted regardless of their sin by the simple laying on of hands.

Number 15: The Greek Fathers

The fourth century had many great leaders. Three Cappadocians from Asia Minor were among the more prominent of the orthodox leaders. Basil was a capable bishop of the metropolitan church of Cæsarea in Cappadocia, and he had the knack of smoothing out theological difficulties. It was he who gave a rule to Eastern monasticism. His brother, Gregory of Nyssa, was the ablest theologian of his party after Athanasius, and he was in close sympathy with the thinking of Origen. The third was Gregory of Nazianzus, a schoolmate of Basil, who became distinguished as a poet and orator. Best known for his reputation as an orator was John Chrysostom, a native of Antioch. He was well educated, passed several years in the austere life of a monk, and then for twelve years was the preacher of the church in Antioch. His practical sermons delighted the people who flocked to hear him. In 398 he was given a still larger role as patriarch of Constantinople. Unfortunately his plain speaking drew the hostility of the empress. His sympathy with the theological position of Antioch invited the hostility of Alexandria also. The result was that he was driven from his see and died in exile.

Impact: The Greek Fathers were important champions and defenders of the Nicene Creed and their influence as men of God who would never waver in their faith did much to defend orthodoxy against heresy and the interference of the government.

Number 16: The Council of Nicea

Theological discussion in about 300 centered on the nature of Christ. While few Christians understood the fine distinctions of the theologians, they sensed the importance of the issue. The author of the Epistle to the Hebrews spoke of him as a high priest who is able to take away human sin. John in his Gospel made Jesus the incarnate Logos. Origen of Alexandria contributed the explanation that Jesus Christ was of the same nature as God. The problem was how to explain Christ so that he would not lose his divine dignity and at the same time keep his human values. The more the deity of Christ was stressed, the greater seemed the danger of making two Gods. The reaction produced Monarchianism, the government of one God. They stated that while on earth Christ's existence as man was a temporary mode of God. This gave them the name of Modalists. Their close identification of the Son with the Father made it possible to charge them with teaching that it was God the Father who suffered on the Cross. Those who liked to emphasize the true humanity of Christ explained that Christ was merely the human Jesus until at his baptism he became the adopted Son of God. These believers were called Dynamic Monarchians. Neither Monarchian theory was a satisfactory explanation of the incarnation. It was difficult to be specific in teaching and escape the accusation of heresy. Such division of forces weakened the Christian Church, and when Constantine decided to make Christianity legal he resolved to unify Christendom. For the West the issue had virtually been settled by Tertullian's teachings on the Trinity. In the East the fourth century brought the debate to a boiling point with the specific argument between Arianism, a form of Monarchianism, and Athanasianism, a form of Catholic theology. The controversy was precipitated by Arius, a presbyter in the church of Alexandria. The dispute between Arius and his bishop, Alexander, was so keen that the Emperor Constantine summoned the Christian bishops to a council at Nicea near his own capital in order to establish unity of doctrine for all the churches. A general council to include all the dignitaries of the Church had never met before. The Council of Nicea, which met in the year 325, ranks as the most important in the history of the Christian Church. An Alexandrian synod had condemned Arius already, but he was supported by Eusebius of Nicomedia and a considerable following. Arius himself was present. Among the supporters of Alexander was Athanasius, at that time a youthful deacon of the church at Alexandria and a few years later its bishop. It was agreed that Jesus was of the same "substance" as the Father and the creed was adopted as orthodox.

Impact: The emperor was pleased with the result and sent Arius and his supporters into banishment. Outside of the Holy Scriptures, the Nicene Creed is the most important document the Church holds to establish orthodoxy.

Number 17: The Council of Constantinople

Soon after the Arian controversy another conflict arose over the person of Christ. The question here was whether the divine nature of Christ absorbed the human, or whether the two remained apart in his person. Again the West was content with the teaching of Tertullian that both natures were complete, but the East was divided by differences of interpretation in the rival schools of Alexandria and Antioch. The Alexandrian school explained the two natures as fused in a single personality; Antioch stressed the separateness of the two natures. Apollinaris, Bishop at Laodicea, thought the true explanation of Christ's nature was that his body and mind were human, but that his spirit was replaced by the Logos.

Impact: Since Apollinaris' doctrine marred the perfection of his humanity, it was condemned at the Council of Constantinople in 381. This same Council asserted the divinity of the Holy Spirit. From that time the Athanasian doctrine of the Trinity has held the orthodox position in Christianity.

Number 18: The Council of Ephesus

The next phase of the controversy was brought about due to statements made by Nestorius, Bishop of Constantinople and a representative of the Antiochian school. Nestorius thought of God as merely dwelling in the human Jesus. Cyril wrote to the Bishop of Rome affirming the Nicene Creed and declaring Nestorian views heretical. The Bishop sided with him, and enlisted the aid of the emperor, Theodosius II. The emperor called a council to settle the matter.

Impact: This third of the ecumenical councils of the Church met at Ephesus in 431 and condemned Nestorius.

Number 19: The Council of Chalcedon
Eutyches, an aged archimandrite at Constantinople, contended that Christ's two natures became one after his incarnation, an opinion which left no room for the human life of Jesus.

Impact: The Council of Chalcedon, the fourth recognized council, in 451 condemned Eutyches. It also recognized the equality of the bishops in Rome and Constantinople.

Number 20: The rise of the Monophysite churches of the Near East
The decision of Chalcedon had far-reaching consequences. The Council, in proclaiming equality between the Bishop of Constantinople and the see of Rome, sowed the seeds of future hostility between East and West. As the representative of the Monophysite principle, the church of Alexandria was dissatisfied with the decision of Chalcedon and dissenting churches arose including the Coptic, the Abyssinian, the Syrian Jacobite, and the Armenian. Armenia had been Christianized as late as the fourth century, and Abyssinia in the same period. Thus the attempts to unify the churches by the councils of Ephesus and Chalcedon had alienated first the Nestorians and then the Monophysites. The unity which Rome created in the West failed in the East. The patriarch of Constantinople was the head of the churches in his own region, but he had no jurisdiction over the schismatic churches. Justinian (527-565) maintained temporarily the prestige of the emperor and established most completely the imperial authority over

the Church. Politically he was successful in reasserting the authority of the empire over Italy and North Africa, which had succumbed to invading Teutonic tribes, though the recovery lasted for only a brief period. Theologically he was sufficiently desirous of winning back the Monophysites and restoring the unity of the Church to call a fifth general council of church leaders. The second Council of Constantinople, in 553, condemned the *Three Chapters* which were the standard of Antiochian theology, and thus favored the Alexandrian interpretation of the creed of Chalcedon, but the attempt to conciliate the Monophysites failed and national churches resulted in disaffected provinces existing throughout the empire.

Impact: The Coptic descendants of the old Egyptians set up a patriarch of their own at Alexandria. He also became the recognized head of the Abyssinian church. Most of the Armenians withdrew from fellowship with the Orthodox and organized their own hierarchy.

Number 21: Benedict writes the first monastic rule
Benedict of Nursia (c. 480-c. 543) studied in Rome but left because of his despair over the corruption he saw. He retired to a cave in seclusion for about three years. In 529 he moved to a remote but beautiful mountain location between Rome and Naples. Here he founded the monastery of Monte Cassino. This effort marked the beginning of monasticism. He presided over the order for 14 years, during which time he composed the Benedictine Rule. The Rule is organized in four parts: at the head of

each monastery is an abbot; vows, including poverty and chastity must be taken; manual labor and education are expected; and in all things simplicity and order must be upheld.

Impact: The Benedictine Rule became the standard upon which all other monastic orders were built and organized.

Number 22: The impact of Islam

The seventh century saw the rise of Mohammedanism when Mohammed made Mecca the center of his new cult. Believing that a new religious era had been established in 622, the year Mohammed fled for his life from Mecca, his followers carried on a militant crusade from country to country throughout the Near East. Their steady progress against all opposition resulted in the loss to the empire of Syria, Palestine, Egypt, North Africa, and Spain. A century later the tide of conquest had swept over the Pyrenees, but the Franks checked the wave of invasion at Tours in 732, saving the West for Christianity. The Eastern Empire was shorn of much of its strength. The Muslim conquests extended as far east as the frontiers of India and China.

Impact: The Empire that centered at Constantinople was so crippled that it could not hope to conquer again any part of Europe, and the patriarch of Constantinople was no longer in a position to rival the Bishop of Rome. The Eastern Church made good some of its losses by sending out missionaries like Cyril and Methodius, winning the allegiance of princes like Boris of Bulgaria and Vladimir of Russia, and asserting the authority of the patriarch of Constantinople over their realms.

Number 23: The Latin Vulgate

Jerome (340-420) was a native of Venetia at the head of the Adriatic Sea. He spent the first part of a long life as a wandering student, visiting many academic centers. Later he lived for a few years at Rome, where he became secretary to Bishop Damasus. At his suggestion Jerome undertook to revise the Latin version of the Gospels. An Old Latin translation had been in use in the provinces of the West since the second century, but all manuscripts had to be copied by hand and errors had crept into them. It was time these were eliminated. Jerome accepted the task and it grew into a new version of the whole Bible. This came to be called the Vulgate, a term that designates it as the people's version, and it remains in use throughout the Roman Catholic Church.

Impact: It was more than eleven hundred years before the Council of Trent gave it official sanction, but usage had confirmed it long before.

Number 24: Fourth and fifth century monasticism

In the fourth and fifth centuries monasticism was becoming popular in the Mediterranean lands. Men and women in growing numbers withdrew and hoped that they would get nearer to God in solitude. At first they went to the outskirts of the inhabited towns, then in their zeal for loneliness they went farther away. Desert regions, especially, became their haunts. The rocks and caves gave them rude shelter. In such places they had ample opportunity to practice the self-denial in which they believed, and the climate lent itself to their austerities without too great hardship. A reputation for saintliness made them the recipients of popular attention and generosity. St. Anthony of Thebes was the best-known representative, and his story caused others to imitate him. Although monasticism was in its inception individualistic, the communal life necessitated discipline over the members. In the fourth century Pachomius had seven thousand monks under his control in Egypt. Basil in Cappadocia regulated the monks of that region with less emphasis on asceticism, and with a recognition of the value of labor and social service as well as of prayer and contemplation.

Impact: Monks cleared forests and built monasteries, setting for the common people an example of industry and morality. They preserved and copied ancient manuscripts, studied the writings of the past, and established monastery schools. Certain of the monks became missionaries to the forest tribes of the North.

Number 25: *The City of God*

The most renowned thinker of the fourth and fifth centuries was Augustine, Bishop of Hippo in North Africa (350-430). Trained at Carthage, he became a teacher at Carthage and Rome, and later was professor of rhetoric at Milan. There he came under the influence of Ambrose, and became a Christian. He had such conviction about personal sin and forgiveness that it shaped his thinking about theology.

During his thirty-five years in the bishopric of Hippo he worked out a system of Latin theology which became the Catholic standard for more than a thousand years. Augustine's insistence on the personal relation of humanity to God made him acceptable even to the Protestants of the sixteenth century. In his *Confessions* Augustine wrote his spiritual autobiography. Convinced of the reality of sin, he felt that his only escape was through the mercy of God. Augustine was also the father of a philosophy of history, set forth in his *City of God*. He lived at a time of political and social upheaval, when the foundations of the Roman Empire were being undermined. The Visigoths sacked the city of Rome in the year 410. Many pagans felt that Rome's misfortunes were the consequence of the neglect of the old gods. Augustine wrote to show that the decline of paganism was due to other causes, and to foretell the triumph of the Christian order in place of the empire whose end was near. He believed that God intended that the Church should rule the State rather than the State the Church.

Impact: Augustine's idea of the *City of God* became the political philosophy of the medieval papacy.

Number 26: The Pelagian controversy

Augustine's greatest contribution to theology was his doctrine of divine control over human destiny. The Greek Fathers maintained that a certain power of free will existed, in contrast to the pagan doctrine of fate. It seemed to them possible that a person could cooperate with God for salvation. But the tendency in the West was to emphasize humanity's fall in Adam and a consequent inability to choose the right. Salvation depended, therefore, on God's willingness to save. Augustine's teaching on election was opposed by Pelagius, a British monk, who claimed that humanity was not helpless in the hands of a partial, predestinating God, but that we have a free will. The Pelagian controversy raged in the Church for a time both in the West and the East. Both decided against Pelagius, but the Church in the East always held that humanity and God could cooperate in human salvation. John Cassian, once a pupil of Chrysostom, and his school in southern Gaul were semi-Pelagian in claiming that humankind has the power to take the initiative in approaching God.

Impact: The Synod of Orange in 529 decreed in favor of Augustine's view. The Roman Catholic Church did not enforce uniformity on these questions, however, as the Eastern councils did.

Number 27: The rise of the Roman church

By the third century the church at Rome enjoyed the highest prestige of any church in Christendom, but as late as the time of Ambrose the Roman bishop was only one among many bishops. The fourth century added to his prestige. In the Donatist schism Constantine turned to the Bishop of Rome to be the mediator. In the Christological controversy the opinion of Rome was important, though not decisive. Bishop Siricius near the end of the fourth century assumed authority to dictate to a Spanish bishop who had written for advice, and suggested that the Spaniard transmit the Roman decision to other bishops in Spain. This authority was recognized by the Emperor Theodosius. In the fifth century Valentinian III decreed the supremacy of Bishop Leo I, giving him power to make law for the whole Western Church. The East, of course, would admit no claims of Rome to supremacy. Leo I may properly be called the first pope, a dignity once used by every local pastor. Leo based his authority on Peter's headship of the Church, and vigorously enforced his claims.

Impact: By the middle of the fifth century the church in Rome had been established as the supreme authority in the West.

Number 28: Invasions from the North

While the Christian church was growing in outward prosperity, the empire was weakening. Economic fortunes were declining as war and pestilence swept away the workers, the families best able to rear children were small in size, taxation was heavy and unjustly distributed, money was scarce, and the whole system of industry rested on slavery and rural serfdom. The irresponsible power of unworthy or inefficient emperors in the third and fourth centuries resulted in despotism and chaos. In 375 the empire of Rome lay along both sides of the Mediterranean Sea from the Atlantic Ocean in the west to the borders of the eastern desert. The Alps protected the peninsula of Italy to the north. Beyond were tribes of barbarians belonging to the German, or Teutonic, race. The territory over which they wandered was a broad plain, which sloped northward to the North and Baltic seas. The people who lived there were hunters and crude farmers. But game was getting scarce, for the lodges of the clansmen were too close together. It was difficult to find sufficient food for the children. The women of the tribes could not raise grain enough on their small cultivated patches of soil to feed so many mouths. Over the southern border were rich provinces of an empire that was growing weak. At last large tribal units began to move. The Visigoths, the Ostrogoths, the Burgundians, the Vandals, the Franks, and others pushed into the lower Danube valley. With slow but relentless progress they traversed the region, then moved up the eastern coast of the Adriatic Sea into the peninsula of Italy. In 410 Rome was sacked.

Impact: The Church was the greatest of the institutions that emerged from this era of confusion. It built up the centralized power of the papacy and extended its influence through missionary activity among the pagan peoples.

Number 29: Gregory I and the medieval papacy

The strength of the Church lay in its leadership, and by the sixth century the supreme leader was the pope of Rome. Gregory I (540-604) was the greatest pope of the medieval papacy. He was city prefect of Rome for a time and for six years served as envoy of the pope at Constantinople. He practiced asceticism in his own home after his return, and was the superior of a family of monks. Upon the death of the sitting pope from the bubonic plague he was elected by the will of the clergy and the people to succeed him. He acted as civil as well as ecclesiastical head, checked the inroads of the last German invaders of Italy, and defended the supremacy of the Roman Church against the Byzantine emperor. The trend of the papacy was toward autocracy, but Gregory liked to speak of himself as "servant of the servants of God." Gregory had a great reputation as a preacher and as a reformer in church music. Aside from his worth as an administrator his greatest contribution to medieval Catholicism was his interpretation of Latin theology and his evangelistic mission to England. Gregory expressed his ideas through his writings as well as in his sermons. They included letters, a bishop's manual, and a commentary on Job.

Impact: Gregory, the first monk to sit on the papal chair, marked the transition from the ancient to the medieval. Appreciative of the old, he preserved orthodoxy while instituting changes that carried the Church forward. He also launched missionary campaigns to unreached barbarians north of the old frontier.

Number 30: Early missions to Ireland and Britain

The evangelization of Ireland and Britain for Christianity was accomplished during the fifth and sixth centuries. Patrick, in his youth a captive among the Irish, returned several years after his escape to extend Christianity there. Monasteries were planted in the country, and Ireland became the base for extensive missions to England and the Continent. In the sixth century Columba, a man of noble lineage among the Irish, founded a monastery on the island of Iona that became the mission center for Britain during the next two hundred years. Chad, a wandering preacher, traveled on foot from the monastery of Lindisfarne to the people of the Midlands until he became known as the Apostle of the Middle English. Hilda was abbess over both monks and nuns at Whitby. Pope Gregory I sent Augustine and a company of monks to convert the Anglo Saxons from heathenism. Augustine arrived at the mouth of the Thames, where the Jutes had landed 150 years earlier, and succeeded in ingratiating himself with the ruler of Kent. Here he established his headquarters at Canterbury. After a time that center became recognized as the headquarters of Roman Christianity and an important school was maintained there.

Impact: The multiplication of churches and schools followed missionary efforts and the English churches were brought into closer contact with the Catholic system on the Continent. Roman Catholic authority later was extended over Ireland and Scotland.

Number 31: Early missions on the European Continent

The Irish monks did not confine their activities to the British Isles. Columbanus (543-615) led a company of twelve monks into Gaul. For a time his revival was popular among the princes as well as the general population. Irish missionaries evangelized and founded monasteries on both sides of the Rhine and beyond in Switzerland and even northern Italy. St. Gall in Switzerland and Bobbio in Italy became famous centers of monastic learning. Eventually leadership passed from the Irish to Roman missionaries. Among these missionaries no one accomplished as much as Boniface. First in pagan Frisia and Thuringia and then into Hesse he wrestled with the pagan customs of the people, built Christian churches, and sent for monks and nuns from England. He was made bishop and then archbishop, and is known in history as the Apostle to the Germans.

Impact: The evangelized tribes were, in many cases, nominal believers who retained many pagan customs. But, over time, churches took root and and Christianity thrived.

Number 32: Early missions to Scandinavia

As the Germans had swarmed southward years earlier, so Norsemen from the Scandinavian peninsula made piratical excursions up the French rivers, seized the district in the north afterwards called Normandy, and wrested eastern England from the Saxon king, Alfred. Other adventurers pushed southeast from Sweden and into Russia where they founded a royal line in the ninth century. The monk Ansgar went to Denmark and Sweden as a missionary and from his diocesan headquarters at Hamburg he was apostolic vicar of the pope over all Scandinavia. But the progress of Christianity was slow. In Norway King Olaf Trigvason was baptized by a hermit, did his best through a short reign to convert his people, and sent missionaries to Iceland and to Greenland. Greenland had a bishop in the tenth century. In the twelfth century Swedish missionaries went into Finland, and each of the three Scandinavian countries eventually had its own bishop.

Impact: In becoming Christians the Norsemen did not lose all of their adventurous spirit, but they came into peaceful relations with continental Europe. Subsequently they formed part of the trading system of the Hanseatic League.

Number 33: The establishment of church courts and canon law

One of the strongest supports of the clergy was the system of ecclesiastical courts. From apostolic times it was an accepted principle that Christians should settle their differences in their own circles rather than resort to the secular courts. As the Church became a social institution with its own interests and property, it was to its advantage to develop its own system of courts, and the civil law of the Roman Empire recognized the right of the Christian Church to do so. In the Middle Ages the legal principles of the Church were superior to those of the State, and offenders preferred to be tried in church courts rather than in civil courts. The bishop's court was the court of principal jurisdiction in the diocese, and all the church courts had their appeal to the papal court at Rome. The elaboration of the ecclesiastical system made necessary a body of canon law. The *Didache* of the second century and the *Didascalia* of the third were tentative attempts to provide regulations for the churches. Out of them was collected the *Apostolic Constitutions* in the fourth century, which contained in eight books a large number of specific liturgical, ethical, and doctrinal precepts.

Impact: In the fifth century an unknown editor compiled the *Apostolic Canons.* In 692 the Second Trullan Council rejected the *Constitutions* but recognized the *Canons,* and thereafter they constituted a part of the collection of canon law.

Number 34: The investiture controversy

Three theories were current during the later Middle Ages regarding the relations between the pope and the German emperor. One was the theory maintained at Rome that the Church was superior to the State and that therefore the emperor had no right to interfere with the papacy. The second was the imperial theory that the State was ordained of God to protect the Church. The third was a theory that each was supreme in its own realm and should work harmoniously with the other. The third seemed impossible to achieve, and for more than a century the champions of the other two principles struggled to win a decisive victory over each other. At a synod held in Rome in 1075 Gregory VII condemned, among other things, lay investiture where a secular ruler could appoint a bishop or priest. But the German emperor, Henry IV, retaliated immediately. He summoned a council of German bishops at Worms, at which the pope was condemned and deposed. Gregory retaliated by excommunicating Henry and pronouncing him deposed. The absurdity of all this was that neither side could carry out the decisions personally against the other. The German people, however, did not support Henry and he was compelled to go in submission to the pope and seek his pardon at Canossa. Here he stood barefoot in the snow of the Apennines until Gregory had satisfied his revenge and let him in.

Impact: Once absolved the emperor hurried home, raised an army and marched on Rome. The pope was aided by the Normans but the contest proved disastrous for Gregory and he died in exile. The quarrel continued until Henry V of Germany compromised with Pope Calixtus II in 1122 and the investiture controversy was settled for a time.

Number 35: The Crusades

In the eleventh century the Seljuk Turks seized Palestine and Asia Minor from the Arabs and the Eastern emperor respectively. Threatened with imminent danger across the Bosporus, the emperor at Constantinople appealed for help to Pope Urban II. The opportunity to expand papal influence prompted the pope to undertake the expulsion of the Turks from the Holy Land. The response was enthusiastic, and in 1096 the enterprise was set in motion and lasted nearly two centuries. Before the First Crusade was organized a horde of peasants led by Peter the Hermit started off but were massacred on the way. Another crowd of two hundred thousand were killed in Hungary. Godfrey of Bouillon and an army of nobles and their followers succeeded in reaching Constantinople and established a feudal principality, called the Latin Kingdom of Jerusalem, and a Latin patriarchate. A second crusade enlisted royal support in France and Germany when the Mohammedans threatened fifty years later to expel the Christians who garrisoned the country, but dissensions ruined the expeditions. A third crusade was deemed necessary when Saladin, prince of the Saracens, wrested the Holy Sepulcher from the Christians in 1187. The kings of England, France, and Germany joined in the expedition, but dissensions arose again and the best they could do was to make a truce with the Mohammedans, which permitted Christians to visit the tomb of Christ and to be exempt from taxation. A fourth expedition plundered Constantinople. The thirteenth century saw the enthusiasm of the crusaders evaporate as other interests drew rulers in new directions. Later crusades did little more than get those involved killed.

Impact: The introduction of feudalism into Palestine resulted in the organization of military orders of knighthood of a semimonastic sort. To the Hospitalers, or Knights of St. John, which had been organized earlier, were added the Templars, who had a house near the site of the Temple in Jerusalem, and the Teutonic Knights, who later distinguished themselves in a crusade against the pagan Prussians of northeastern Europe. Out of such knightly orders sprang chivalry, the flower of feudalism in Europe.

Number 36: Anselm and the doctrine of the atonement

The principal contribution to Christian thought made between 500 and 1200 was Anselm's doctrine of the atonement of Christ. Augustine's emphasis on the divine will and on the part of the Church in salvation left the actual achievement by Christ relatively unimportant. The common conception of the atonement was that the death of Jesus served as a ransom to free humanity from bondage to Satan. Anselm, primate of the English church in about 1100, held that men and women had dishonored God by their disobedience, and God demanded a satisfaction which humanity was unable to give. Humans must therefore die and suffer the penalties for their sins unless someone else could pay the debt. Christ was able to do this because he was both man and God, and could more than pay any human debt by his excess of merit.

Impact: The emphasis of Anselm on Christ's part in the atonement did not lessen the importance of the Church so the bishops had little quarrel with him. His theory of the atonement gained general acceptance.

Number 37: The rise of the Schoolmen

Learning was handicapped throughout the Middle Ages by the authority of ecclesiastical tradition. A permanent set of ideas was supported by medieval institutions, and no individual might rationalize independently. Peter Abelard was a brilliant exception. Born in Brittany about 1080, of noble family, he left his home to become a wandering scholar. He loved to debate questions of philosophy by means of the dialectical method of Aristotle's logic. He raised troublesome questions, presenting arguments on both sides of an issue, and invited his students to draw their own conclusions. In a Latin book entitled *Sic et Non* he ventured to raise questions about the fundamentals of theology. Eventually he was forced to recant his teachings. For the next century the Church was suspicious of Aristotle, but it could not stem the tide of his popularity. The Schoolmen have been called the first of the modernists because they submitted their theology to the test of reason. For a while they tried to prove their faith by their reason, but they found that impossible in its entirety. Thomas Aquinas eventually made the distinction between natural religion, which reason approves, and revealed religion, which only insight and faith can grasp.

Impact: Clergy who became Schoolmen were suspected by the Church of heresy, yet they were only trying to understand the Christian teachings that had been handed down from the ancient Church and to justify it by their reason. Even Thomas Aquinas did not escape the charge of introducing dangerous doctrines, though he became the accepted master of Catholic theology. They did not intend to overstep the bounds of authority, but they mark the beginning of the modern tendency toward critical thought directed toward even the most sacred themes of Christian tradition.

Number 38: The establishment of universities

As thoughtful minds became restless over questions the Schoolmen proposed they began to come together for discussion. This is how universities sprang up. Originally the university was neither an educational institution nor a collection of buildings. The first university was a guild of students at Bologna, organized for the protection of the students from the local townspeople. Later it came to include all the students there. At Paris, where a number of teachers set up a school of dialectic, they formed a university organization which became a model for later universities. Even then it was only a guild. Some of the universities were an outgrowth of monastic schools, others an enlargement of lay schools. At first there was no system or discipline but eventually recognition of both students and teachers became necessary and, for purposes of regulation, a system of degrees became organized. Later the universities attained permanency by erecting buildings and libraries which were funded through public or private donations.

Impact: Though the universities held to accepted philosophy and theology, some of them became centers of progressive thought. Out of the universities came all the great reformers and progressive leaders including John Wycliffe at Oxford, Martin Luther at Wittenberg, John Calvin at Geneva, and John and Charles Wesley at Oxford.

Number 39: The rise of nationalism

Until the thirteenth century every lord was able to carry on warfare against another if he saw fit, and every city could be aggressive if it preferred. National governments were overshadowed by the medieval empire and the medieval Church. The real political awakening came with a nationalistic uprising against the temporal authority of the papacy. It was the arrogance of the papacy that brought this about. The Church used various means to take money from the people to meet its lavish expenses. Papal legates provoked popular indignation in different quarters because of their arrogance and greed. No open opposition broke out until near the close of the thirteenth century, however. Late in the thirteenth century France and England found themselves at war and in need of money. The Church in each country claimed immunity from taxation, though it had extensive lands in both. When the kings ventured to demand money from the clergy, the pope refused. The King of France, Philip the Fair, made the quarrel a national issue and rallied the people about himself. Soon French emissaries went to Rome to tell Boniface VIII in person that he was no longer the overlord of France. Meanwhile King Edward I demanded a contribution from the clergy to help wage war against France. In 1366 England refused to pay the papal tribute any longer. Soon Germany joined the rebellion against Rome when, in 1338 at a meeting of the German electors, it was declared that the emperor, not the pope, was divinely ordained to rule Germany. Marsiglio, a canon of Padua in Italy, wrote an influential pamphlet called *Defensor Pacis*. Here he stated that Christ exercised no coercive jurisdiction and neither should the pope. Soon the idea of a secular sovereign became accepted in Europe.

Impact: With the spirit of nationalism came the rise of absolute monarchs like the Tudors and the Bourbons whose sole interests were in maintaining their power rather than advancing the cause of the Church.

Number 40: The Inquisition

The Fourth Lateran Council impressed upon the bishops the responsibility of hunting out heresy. It was decided that it was better to take the life of a heretic rather than let his or her soul suffer eternal punishment. In the Middle Ages torture was an accompaniment of judicial trials, and it was applied freely to extort confessions of heresy. As confessions increased, it was deemed necessary to establish a special tribunal for the trial of heresy cases, and the Inquisition was firmly established in 1252. This gradually became a system of courts under papal control, with an inquisitor-general as chief administrator. The system included salaried officials at local points and the civil assistance of secular officials. Persons were arrested on suspicion and compelled to prove their innocence. If convicted their property was confiscated and the proceeds were divided among the court officials, the bishops, and the civil powers. Confession of guilt might readmit the indicted person to the privileges of the Church, but he or she must suffer long imprisonment as a punishment. If they did not confess they were turned over to the civil authorities who promptly burned them alive.

Impact: The persecution of so-called heretics had unfortunate results. It brutalized the people and destroyed some of the great figures in the Church. It also alienated many Catholics and caused economic loss from the destruction of property and enforced emigration.

Number 41: The influence the friars

Monasticism was based on the principle that a religious life could not be lived in the midst of the world's activities. Friars, instead, found their religious expression in the social life of their times. Rather than isolated contemplation they strove toward evangelism and social service. The friars found their lives by losing them, as Jesus did, in service to others. Two influential friars were Francis of Assisi and Dominic. Wedded to the "Lady Poverty," Francis worked among lepers, befriended the sick and the needy, and preached wherever he went. Pope Innocent III sanctioned a new brotherhood around Francis and it speedily won a popularity that the old orders could not equal. While Francis was initiating the Franciscan order, Dominic, a Spanish theologian, devoted his life to the suppression of such heresies as he saw in southern France. Convinced that the parish priests were not capable of coping with heretics, he organized an order of black-robed friars to go forth and preach and suppress heresy. He too received the sanction of the pope, and the Dominicans became rivals of the Franciscans in the universities and in the esteem of the people. The popularity of the movement led to the organization also of Carmelites and Augustinians.

Impact: The movement in general stimulated religion, and in spite of later degeneracy was evidence of a desire for a more vital kind of religion.

Number 42: The growing discontent with the papacy
The fourteenth century saw renewed discontent against the papacy. William of Occam, an English Schoolman, attacked the papacy as the ultimate authority in religion and demanded that people rely on the Scriptures instead. In England John Wycliffe called into question leading doctrines of Catholicism. He was a graduate of Oxford University who later became a teacher at the school. Since he held that the Bible rather than the pope was the ultimate authority in all spiritual matters he made an English translation from the Latin Vulgate in the common vernacular. Not many copies were made but a number of them survived, despite the determined efforts of the Catholic Church to destroy them. He sent out companies of russet-gowned priests who accepted his leadership to preach his ideas throughout the cities and the countryside. His followers were known as Lollards. Wycliffe has been called the last of the Schoolmen and the "morning star of the Reformation."
Impact: Wycliffe's Bible must be counted among the many causes behind the Reformation in England.

Number 43: Reforms among the Bohemian clergy
Under the influence of Wycliffe, a reform movement spread among the Bohemian clergy. Of note was John Hus, a student at the university of Prague who saw Wycliffe as a role model. He studied the Bible earnestly and declared that unworthy priests should not be permitted to administer the sacraments. He was summoned to defend

himself against the charge of heresy at the Council of Constance in 1415, where he was condemned and burned at the stake for heresy.

Impact: The death of Hus was resented bitterly by the Bohemians and led to a long war with the German Empire, a conflict that was both national and religious in character. Inspired by Hus, anti-Catholic church groups like the Bohemian Brethren and the Waldensians produced vernacular translations of Scripture and their aggressive evangelism won many converts to their cause.

Number 44: The Great Schism

In the late fourteenth century the papal seat was moved to Avignon. The subservience of the papacy to France alienated both England and Germany and tales of debauchery shocked and demoralized the laity. The pope was urged by faithful leaders to return to Rome, advice Gregory XI took in 1377. Unfortunately the return was very displeasing to a corrupt faction of the clergy, and the next year they took the radical step of electing another pope. For the next thirty-six years, until the Council of Constance met in 1414, this Great Schism, as it was called, could not be healed. The national leaders of Europe fell on both sides of the issue as seemed to their advantage. The people steadily lost respect for popes who hurled curses at each other.

Impact: Three councils met one after another in an attempt to bring order out of chaos and to reform the Church. These three are called the Reforming Councils, and they constitute an important chapter in the history of the first half of the fifteenth century.

Number 45: The first printing press

Johann Gutenberg (c. 1400-1468)The inventor of movable type and the father of printing is, ironically, a man of mystery with very little information about his life known for certain. He was born in Mainz, Germany and later his family moved to Strasbourg. In about 1438 he became a printer, returned to Mainz, and developed a partnership with a wealthy gold merchant named Johann Fust. They began a printing press and their first book, a Latin Bible known as the "Gutenberg Bible," was completed in about 1456. Around this same time Fust filed a lawsuit against Gutenberg to recover the money he had invested and Gutenberg was forced to relinquish his share of the business. He continued to dabble in various printing endeavors but died a pauper.

Impact: Gutenberg's advances in printing technology allowed Bible translators to make the Scriptures available to the common person, a primary catalyst behind the success of the Reformation.

Number 46: The Renaissance

From the fourteenth to the sixteenth centuries the Renaissance marked a rebirth of interest in classical Greek literature and art and promoted an ideal of humanism. Although the Renaissance produced among certain elites a religious indifference that began to undermine ecclesiastical authority, soon even the popes became enamored with Renaissance ideas. Nicholas V, for instance, was trained in humanism and carried its ideas into the Vatican. He tried to beautify religion with art and he collected the books that became the foundation for the Vatican Library. Old buildings were restored, and architectural marvels were erected. Art blossomed with amazing opulence and musical achievements soared. The Renaissance took on a more religious character in France, Germany, and England where scholars turned the new world of the classical languages and documents into a better understanding of the Bible. The invention of printing by movable type was an important means of diffusing Renaissance ideas.

Impact: The Renaissance transformed the way scholars, artists, and philosophers viewed the world. It had no immediate impact on the common people, however.

Number 47: The sale of indulgences sparks the Reformation

Deep as were the underlying causes of the Reformation its outbreak was precipitated by the simple need to repay a debt. Albert, a young cleric, had been appointed archbishop of Mainz, and needed many thousand gulden to pay for the woolen scarf which the pope gave to an archbishop as his badge of office. He arranged with the Fugger banking house of Augsburg to supply the money with the understanding that the pope, who wanted as much as he could get from the transaction for the special purpose of building St. Peter's at Rome, should sanction a sale of indulgences in Germany. An indulgence was a draft upon the bank of heaven to pay for sin. It was an axiom of the Catholic faith that sin could be forgiven by the priest in the name of God, but the penalties for sin were still to be paid. The sinner must suffer after death unless by penance he or she could appease God and have the punishment settled. It was a teaching of the Church that the death of Jesus had heaped up a treasury of merit upon which the Church was privileged to draw drafts. Such a draft was a pardon that removed the penalty. It cost the sinner money to obtain this pardon and there were unscrupulous clergy who sold them at a high price, even declaring that such a document could be obtained before the sin was committed. The particular sale that was arranged in Germany was progressing favorably in 1517, when John Tetzel, the sales agent in the neighborhood of Wittenberg in Saxony, sold a few indulgences to persons from that town. When they confessed their sins next time to Martin Luther and presented their pardons as acquitting them of penance he was troubled. Luther was a Saxon friar who had been studying the Bible with a growing conviction that Catholic faith and practice were mistaken at many points. Believing that indulgences were a travesty on the forgiving grace of God and a financial curse to his own country of Germany, he wrote out a series of arguments, or theses, on the subject in Latin and posted them on the bulletin board of the university. He hoped that they might arouse discussion of the subject among the learned doctors of the Church. The theses were translated into German, printed, and scattered widely however. Luther declared that people were justified in the sight of God by personal faith in Christ rather than by any expensive scheme or work of merit. It is little wonder that Luther's convictions were widely hailed.

Impact: Luther's contempt for injustice and oppression and his love for God's Word and the freedom it offered launched the Protestant Reformation. It was the simple sale of indulgences, however, that inspired him to nail his written protest in a public forum.

Number 48: The life of Martin Luther

Luther, a miner's son, was born in Eisleben in 1483. Though of humble birth, he was able to attend the University of Erfurt, where he expected to complete his training for the law. But while there he was driven by circumstances to choose the life of a monk and he entered a cloister of the Augustinian friars in Erfurt. Here he began to study the Bible and saw that the emphasis of the Church upon deeds of merit was false security for salvation, and that personal faith in Christ as Savior could alone justify the sinner before God. He secured a position to teach in the new University of Wittenberg, and there became involved after a time in the indulgence controversy. During the next few years Luther wrote and spoke with increasing independence. He criticized the Church. He wrote pamphlets to prove his points and as a means of popular appeal in a time when there were no newspapers to shape public opinion. At first the pope was disposed to laugh at a squabble between Augustinian and Dominican friars, but the Augustinian order to which Luther belonged was told to take him in hand. Luther met with his brothers in convention at Heidelberg but gained more there than he lost. He was indicted and summoned to Rome for trial but through the friendship of his prince, Frederick, the Elector of Saxony, the trial was held in German territory at Augsburg where Luther had a hearing before a papal legate. This did not end the matter, and the disturbance was so alarming in Saxony that the pope sent a representative to find out the exact situation. A debate followed with John Eck, a Catholic champion, in which Luther was forced to admit that he agreed with John Hus, who had been condemned by the Council of Constance a century earlier and Luther was excommunicated from the Church. In 1521 the Emperor Charles convened a legislative diet of the empire at Worms on the Rhine. Luther was summoned to attend by an imperial herald. The grave question was whether the German government would carry out the papal condemnation. Before all the dignitaries of the empire, lay and clerical, and before the papal legate, Luther was asked whether he stood by the position that he had taken in his writings. He declared that he took his stand on the Bible as his authority and refused to recant what he had written, unless it could be proved false by the Scriptures. The emperor forced an edict of condemnation through the Diet and Luther was made an outlaw. It was then that Luther's friends seized him under cover of night and carried him for safety to the castle of the Wartburg, where he remained for a year. This gave him opportunity for further study, and here he commenced his German translation of the Bible. Other vernacular German translations from the Latin Vulgate had preceded it, but Luther used the colloquial language of the people and translated from the original with the help of the best critical texts. The result was a German Bible that became the accepted version of the German Protestants, and fixed the form of the literary language of the country. In the years that followed Luther wrote and preached many sermons, he wrote expositions of the books of the Bible, he was the author of hymns that he published for the use of the people, and he had a wide correspondence.

Impact: Much of the history of the Reformation depends on the ideas of Martin Luther. Because of him the revolt was more ecclesiastical than theological, except in the fundamental difference of Protestant dependence on faith for salvation and Catholic dependence on the sacraments of the Church. The basic principle on which Luther based his reconstruction of theology was that individual salvation from sin and its punishment was to be obtained by personal faith in Christ as a sufficient Savior rather than faith in the priest, the sacraments, and the whole system of Catholicism.

Number 49: The Peasants' War

The Lutheran movement brought into the open certain radical tendencies, both religious and social. The rural peasants had more than once broken into rebellion locally against the hard conditions of their lot. They hoped that the revolt against the Church might go farther and emancipate them from their feudal obligations to ecclesiastical and lay lords. An uprising resulted in the Peasants' War in 1524. There was much lawlessness and some loss of life, but the reprisals were more severe than the rebels deserved. They demanded little more than the right to the old medieval communal claims, but they were feared as socialists, promptly punished for their temerity by ruthless slaughter, and forced back into submission.

Impact: The most serious consequence of the uprising was the effect upon Luther. It drove him back upon his natural conservatism, made him fear the effects of radicalism upon his own movement, and turned him away from the principle of individual rights. From that time Luther was more disposed to give to the State the direction of religion.

Number 50: The Anabaptists

The Anabaptists were the heirs of the evangelical spirit of the German brethren. Stirred by the Lutheran movement, they were more disposed to follow Luther's example of independent action, though they were not ready to join his movement. With a literal interpretation of the Bible they reached certain conclusions that were quite unconventional. They were dubbed Anabaptists because they rebaptized those who joined their company, and they refused baptism to infants on the ground that they were not old enough to have conscious faith. They chose their own religious leaders and organized tentatively on a presbyterian basis, rejecting the authority of the Catholic

Church. Two men represented divergent types of Anabaptism. Balthasar Hübmaier was their leader in theological disputation. John Denck represented the prevalence of their mysticism and is related in his spiritual attitude to the later Quakers of England, as Hübmaier anticipated the English Baptists. Lutherans and Catholics alike opposed them. But Anabaptists persisted in the Netherlands, where they took the name of Mennonites from their leader Menno Simons.

Impact: In general the Anabaptists were peaceful and drew disaffected persons of various sorts. Yet, while it was primarily a religious movement, it included some who were fanatical in their anticipation of the second coming of Christ and who were eager to hurry it along.

Number 51: The Swiss Reformation

In 1519, two years after Luther published his theses, Ulrich Zwingli was made priest of the church at Zurich. He had been born a few weeks after Luther and was educated at Basle, Berne, and Vienna. He had also made many friends among the humanists. He was attracted to a clerical life because of its opportunities for study, and initially he became parish priest at Glarus. Later his friends secured him the appointment to Zurich. In time he became hostile in his attitude toward the requirements of the Catholic religion. He opposed the ascetic life, saint worship, and the belief in purgatory. He accepted the Bible as the supreme authority in religion, and Christ as a sufficient Savior. He preached these as theological truths, but he was morally lax, and did not know religion by personal experience. Illness sobered him, and he became interested in bringing about reforms in the city. By 1523 he was debating before the city council and in public the abolition of images in the churches, and contending that the Lord's Supper was only a memorial of Jesus. As a consequence the council abolished images, the mass, and the monasteries. Morals courts were set up to take the place of the church courts in cases of conduct and marriage. Zwingli became the power behind the council. He was different from Luther in his outlook on life, in his religious experience, in his aims, and in his methods. Luther was naturally conservative, hoping to save what he could of the old system unless the Bible discredited it. Zwingli wanted to do away with every practice that the Bible did not specifically mention. Zwingli was also a patriot who was ready to fight for his political principles. Thus the troubles he got into came from the Catholic cantons, which threatened war on Zurich, not the pope who saw Zwingli as a minor player. The Swiss Confederation was segregated into two groups: the states that desired democratic government, moral and ecclesiastical reforms, and the abolition of mercenary customs and those that were aristocratic in politics, loyally Catholic, and inclined to hold on to foreign pensions and military payments. War broke out and Zwingli's Zurich army was defeated at Kappel in 1531. Zwingli was killed in the battle.

Impact: Zwingli's mantle of leadership fell to Heinrich Bullinger, a friend of John Calvin and a man whose temperate nature brought various groups together and helped further the Reformation in Switzerland.

Number 52: The Reformation in French Switzerland
The Reformation came to Geneva through the preaching of William Farel, an heir of the French nobility. Because of his radical tendencies he was not permitted to preach in France, and he went to Basle, where he became active in religious discussion. There he organized a church of French Protestant refugees, but he was too restless to remain long in one place. He ultimately went to Geneva, the gateway from Switzerland into France. In 1504 a political revolt had given the city independence from its Catholic bishop and Luther's books had set the stage for religious changes when Farel came to the city. He became a recognized Protestant leader, but he did not possess the ability to organize the movement. Realizing his limitations, he seized an opportunity to enlist John Calvin, a French refugee who was in the city temporarily. Quite unexpectedly Calvin found himself drafted to lead an enterprise which became as widely known and as influential as the German movement of Luther. A French Reformer and theologian, Calvin was the son of a lawyer who planned for him to become a priest. In 1523 he began studies at the University of Paris until his father changed his mind and sent him to the University of Orleans to study law. After his father's death in 1531 he abandoned law and went to Paris to study humanities. Here he had a "sudden conversion," as he would later describe it, and left the Catholic Church to

become a Protestant leader and preacher. His outspokenness and brilliant mind got him in trouble in Paris so he and a companion, Nicholas Cop, left the city; eventually ending up in Strasbourg. Here, in 1536, he published *Institutes of the Christian Religion*, which stressed the sovereignty of God, a limited atonement, predestination, and irresistible grace. His travels took him to Geneva, Switzerland where he eventually, after a series of conflicts with the Catholic leadership and others, established the city as the "Rome of Protestantism." He ran the city with strict authority and engaged in organizing nearly every aspect of its civic affairs. He remained here until his death.

Impact: Calvin's influence can be seen to this day in the various denominations that embrace his theology, including Presbyterian and Reformed churches.

Number 53: The Scottish Reformation

In Scotland prior to the Reformation immoral conduct among the clergy was worse than in most countries. In time they provoked reaction in Scotland as elsewhere. Protestant influences began to seep through from the Continent by way of trade routes and the universities. Books and pamphlets, ballads and plays, teaching and preaching, had each sown seeds of religious revolt. Parliamentary prohibitions of Protestant literature were ineffective. Patrick Hamilton, a university-bred Scotch noble, gave his life for the faith. George Wishart was another convert who preached until he too was seized, tried, and burned. A companion of Wishart on his preaching tours was John Knox. Born in Haddington, Scotland and educated at the University of Glasgow, Knox was originally a Roman Catholic priest. In 1543 he converted to Protestantism and spread the message of the Reformation until his capture by the French in 1547 when they attacked Saint Andrews. He was forced to labor in a French galley for almost two years until Edward VI, the king of England, secured his release. He moved to England and became the royal chaplain in 1551. When Catholic Queen Mary took the throne in 1553 he fled to Frankfurt and later to Geneva. Here he met Calvin and began studying his doctrines. He preached widely throughout Europe for a number of years until his return to Scotland in 1559. He denounced the Catholic Church and Scotland's Catholic regent, Mary of Guise. He supported the Protestant revolt against the regency, a hopeless cause until England's Elizabeth I, who had succeeded her half-sister Mary, agreed to support them. After the death of Mary of Guise, the Protestants took control of the Scottish government and Knox's Confession of Faith was adopted by the Parliament. Control was lost briefly upon the return of yet another Catholic Mary, Mary Stuart, who reigned from 1560 to 1567. She had Knox arrested for treason, although he was later acquitted. He spent his remaining years after Mary's death preaching and writing.

Impact: From Scotland, Calvinism was spread around the world through aggressive missions activities.

Number 54: The English Reformation

When the Lutheran revolt occurred in Germany England's King Henry VIII wrote against the movement. The pope was pleased and gave the king the title of "Defender of the Faith." Things fell apart when he fell for Anne Boleyn, a maid of honor of Queen Catherine of Aragon, whom he had married for the sake of an alliance with Spain. Because the special consent of the pope had been required for the marriage, a papal dispensation was necessary for an annulment. The pope was unwilling to grant the annulment because of how it would impact his relationship with the Emperor Charles V, who was Catherine's nephew. Cardinal Wolsey, Henry's minister, was unable to get the pope's consent and in his impatience Henry declared himself the head of the Church in England and got the divorce through an English court. By this act of rebellion from Rome Henry rejected the ecclesiastical authority of the papacy. This change of headship of the English Church, however, did not mean that England became Protestant. It was in effect a nationalization of the Catholic Church. But it proved to be the first step in a series which in the end would take England away from its Catholic allegiance. Even the forceful policy of the king might not have carried the nation with him had it not been for other forces that were at work to undermine Catholicism. The remaining influence of Wycliffe and his Bible was one of these. A second was the effect of the Lutheran movement and of the writings of Luther, which found their way to England in spite of their blacklisting by Church authorities. A third influence were men like William Tyndale, translator of the first modern English Bible, and John Colet, an Oxford professor who used the New Testament as a basis for his lectures. A fourth cause was the popular dissatisfaction with the immorality of the priests and bishops for it was plain that the Church was squeezing all the money possible out of the pockets of the people.

Impact: The cumulative effect of these various influences prepared the public mind for Henry's act of rebellion. Parliament was submissive enough to the king's will to ratify his action and vote him the title of Supreme Head of the Church of England. It transferred to him the power of appointment of the higher clergy. Appeals to Rome were abolished and the dispensing power was given to the Archbishop of Canterbury. By these specific acts the separation from Rome was made complete by 1535.

Number 55: The influence of Thomas Cranmer

Henry made Thomas Cranmer, who was sympathetic to Lutheranism, Archbishop of Canterbury. His first task was to produce the Ten Articles of Religion. Five of them were doctrinal in nature including authorizing the use of the Bible, reaffirming the three great creeds, and setting the decisions of the first four ecumenical councils as standards. The other five articles were ceremonial. The Articles were published in the king's name, and with them a set of Royal Injunctions, directing the clergy in the use of the Articles and the Bible. The Injunctions gave practical advice to the parish priests about conducting worship services and instructing the people in religious fundamentals. Henry authorized the public use in the churches of a recent Bible translation which Matthew Coverdale had made on the basis of Tyndale's translation. Yet, the people were not satisfied with the Ten Articles or the Bible so Henry and Cranmer tried again with Thirteen Articles, and this time the influence of the Augsburg Confession was apparent.

Impact: The death of Henry in 1547 made it possible for Cranmer and King Edward VI to carry the ecclesiastical changes farther. Cranmer directed the clergy to read the Ten Commandments and the Lord's Prayer weekly in the churches, together with a chapter from the Old Testament and another from the New. A new edition of the Bible, known as the Great Bible, was placed in every church, and the priests were supplied with homilies for popular instruction. The organization of the church was left virtually unchanged, however. The two archbishops of Canterbury and York remained under the pope, and the episcopal arrangement of bishops was not abolished. The king continued to be the head of the Church and made the appointments of bishops and archbishops.

Number 56: The recovery of English Catholicism

With Edward's early death in 1553 his older sister Mary became queen. There was a brief attempt to place Lady Jane Grey on the throne but the people wanted their rightful sovereign, the daughter of Catherine of Aragon. She was a loyal Catholic and she promptly restored Catholicism and sought the forgiveness of the pope. Cardinal Pole, Mary's best friend in England, was made papal legate and absolved the nation. Most of the people cared little whether Catholic England was under papal or royal jurisdiction, but many liked the old Catholic ways and there was no disturbance over the changes in religion that Mary made. The leaders in the Church of England were divided in their preferences. Men like Gardiner, whom Mary made Lord Chancellor, and Bonner, Bishop of London, would have been content with royal instead of papal supremacy, and Cranmer preferred Protestantism, but the queen had her way. Gardiner and Bonner fell in with her policies. Cranmer went to the stake, and with him were burned Latimer and Ridley, both eminent scholars, because they would not conform to the Catholic policy of Mary.

Impact: The short and unhappy reign of "Bloody Mary" resulted in the execution of about three hundred persons. She was disappointed in her marriage to Philip II of Spain and was disappointed in her hope of an heir. Her death after five years on the throne was celebrated in England and the people gladly welcomed her half sister, Elizabeth.

Number 57: The Elizabethan era

Elizabeth's 45-year reign is one of the outstanding epochs of English history. She molded the English church by restoring the reforms made by Cranmer when Parliament, by the Act of Supremacy, gave the queen similar control of religion as her father had enjoyed, but with the title of Governor of the Church of England. With certain reservations the Prayer Book compiled during Edward's reign was adopted and the revised Thirty-nine Articles became the norm of faith. The queen appointed new bishops and made Matthew Parker, her former tutor, Archbishop of Canterbury. In Parker Elizabeth had an archbishop who would further Protestantism including the highly popular usage of Psalm singing.

Impact: Elizabeth's popularity and the skill of men like Parker helped ensure the permanent establishment of Protestantism in Britain, although there were still many bumps in the road ahead.

Number 58: English Catholics and Separatists

No ecclesiastical decision would please all the people because the Reformation encouraged differences of opinion. John Jewel, the bishop of Salisbury, was a representative of those who believed in a national Protestant Church. An exile during Mary's reign because he would not attend mass, he returned to write an *Apology for the Anglican Church*, which gave him a reputation abroad and was so acceptable in England that it was distributed among the parish churches. In his book he maintained the antiquity of the Anglican religion as older than Roman Catholicism. Elizabeth found herself between two extreme factions, neither of which was pleased with the decisions of the queen. The Catholics, disappointed over her failure to approve the old religion, plotted to replace Elizabeth with Mary, Queen of Scots. They accepted invitations to meet secretly in the houses of the faithful for mass and welcomed Jesuit priests from France. On the other hand were Separatists like the Puritans, whose leaders had mostly been exiles at Geneva during Mary's reign. At first they applauded the changes that the queen made, but they were not satisfied when she refused to go further. They wished to purge the church of all Catholic influences. One third of the 98 clergymen in London gave up their livings and renounced their Anglican membership. Thomas Cartwright, a professor at Cambridge, became recognized as the chief exponent of Puritanism, but not all Puritans were ready to follow his desire to abolish bishops in favor of presbyteries. Most Puritans preferred to stay in the Church of England, if possible, but they wished to improve it.

Impact: Neither the Catholics nor the Separatists could gain a strong foothold and many came to the New World where they could more successfully and easily practice their religion.

Number 59: The Society of Jesus

During the Protestant Reformation that occupied the nations of the East and West, the peoples of southern Europe remained true to the old Catholic order. Yet, even here, there was a desire among many for reform in the Church. For example, Cardinal Ximenes of Spain sympathized with the desire of Queen Isabella for certain reforms. As head of the Church in Spain, he was able to provide better training for the clergy. The most efficient agency in the Catholic recovery was the Society of Jesus, or the Jesuits. The Jesuits owed their inspiration to Loyola who, like Luther, had passed through a conflict of religious emotions, nearly losing his sanity in his efforts to get near to God. Unlike Luther, though, Loyola's experience made him inwardly more intense, and he resolved to conquer the mysteries of religion. He disciplined himself by a set of "spiritual exercises" and resolved to found a new Catholic order which should serve as a standing army for the defense of the Roman Catholic Church. Selecting a few of his fellow students he formed the Society of Jesus, which in 1540 received the sanction of the pope. Almost from the time of the formation of the society missionaries went out to Asia and French Canada. Instead of withdrawing from the world their task was to mold the world for Catholicism. Members were graded according to their length of service and proficiency, with an inner circle that chose the officers and administered the detailed affairs of the order. It was a marvelously efficient machine.

Impact: Almost at once the Jesuits leaped to a position of leadership in the councils of the Church. As missionaries and as heresy hunters they were absolutely devoted to their purpose. They did much to save southern Europe for the Catholic Church. Yet the Jesuits were also charged with encouraging superstition and the order became so distrusted and disliked that it was suppressed in one country after another until Pope Clement XIV abolished the order in 1773 – a decision later reversed by Pope Pius VII.

Number 60: The Council of Trent

In 1545 a Catholic council was called to respond to the Protestant Reformation. It became an 18 year process that defined essential dogmas for the Church. The statements of the Council of Trent lacked clarity, but it adhered to the seven sacraments, authorized officially the use of the Vulgate Bible of Jerome (which had been used unofficially for nearly twelve centuries), and reaffirmed the equal authority of tradition with Scripture. Various commissions were appointed to carry out needed measures. One of the most important was the Congregation of the Index for the censorship of religious literature, which drew up a blacklist of offensive publications. A Tridentine Creed was prepared which contained the Nicene statements, a summary of the decrees of Trent, and a confession of the primacy of the pope.

Impact: Pius IV confirmed the decrees of the council in 1564 and they set the standard of faith for the Catholic Church until the mid-20th century.

Number 61: The Jansenists

The Jansenists were a group of scholarly men who came into prominence in France because of their opposition to the Jesuits. Among Catholics they filled the place of the contemporary Puritans as critics, but they were too intellectual to get much of a following and they lacked the stern moral purpose and force that made the Puritan movement so potent. Cornelius Jansen, a bishop in Belgium in the early seventeenth century, studied Augustine and

started a controversy with the Jesuits by charging them with denying predestination and holding the doctrine and the moral principles of Pelagius. Other scholars rallied around Jansen. The pope condemned his teachings and many Jansenists bowed to the decision. Yet the Jesuits sought revenge and the Jansenists scattered for their safety.
Impact: The Jansenists spread and maintained a presence in certain parts of Europe until the 1760s when their influence helped purge the Jesuits from France. After this triumph their numbers steadily declined.

Number 62: The Thirty Years War

The Thirty Years' War broke out because neither Catholics nor Protestants would honestly keep the terms of the Peace of Augsburg agreed upon in 1555. After that peace the Lutherans were aggressive and continued to lay hands upon all church property that they could get and to hold it. Catholics resented this and recovered all that they could as they began to win back parts of Germany. Had it not been for fear of one another, and because of the peaceable disposition of the reigning emperors of Germany, war might have come sooner than it did. In 1608 a Protestant Union was formed followed by a Holy League of the Catholics the next year. The League was much more closely knit together than the loosely organized Protestant Union, and the Protestant cause continued to suffer because of the rivalries for leadership among the princes. It was ten years longer before war actually occurred. The characteristics of the war were the widening circles of states that became involved, and the intermingling of religious and political interests.

Impact: The net result of the war was to bring peace between the various interests, but at the cost of frightful suffering and enormous loss of life. Sheer exhaustion led finally to peace. The treaty which was arranged after prolonged negotiation brought to an end the long wars of religion in central Europe, and virtually marks the end of the period of the Reformation.

Number 63: The Armenian Controversy

Differences in doctrine developed similarly in the Netherlands. The Dutch provinces had won their independence when a truce was agreed upon with Spain in 1609. In spite of the struggle for existence the country had prospered. Manufacturing and commerce made great strides, and populations increased. Dutch sailors rivaled the English on all the seas. Dutch Protestantism was of the Calvinistic type, and Calvinistic doctrine was taught in the universities. In 1602 Jacob Arminius became a professor in the University of Leyden. A colleague charged him with being lukewarm in his attitude toward the doctrine of predestination and an investigation followed. This aroused discussion and a national synod was planned to settle the controversy, when Arminius suddenly died. His sympathizers then issued a Remonstrance, appealing to the provincial governments of Holland and Friesland for toleration. In their statement they opposed five items among the famous five points of Calvinism. They modified the theory of unconditional election of certain human beings by the sovereign will of God by saying that election was based on the divine foreknowledge of a person's faith. They asserted that the atonement of Christ was not limited to the few elect but was universal in its scope for all who would accept it. Instead of affirming human helplessness they believed in spiritual regeneration. Over against the doctrine of divine grace as irresistible they set the resistibility of salvation. And where the Calvinist insisted on the perseverance of the elect, Arminians were doubtful about perseverance. At last in 1618 the long awaited Synod met at Dort. Eighty-four theologians and numerous secular officials composed its membership. Only three Arminians were present, and they were dismissed after a plea for toleration.

Impact: The Synod published ninety-three canons and endorsed the Belgic Confession of 1561 and the Heidelberg Catechism. The Remonstrants were required to accept the canons, give up their churches, and retire from the country. After a few years milder counsels prevailed and some of them found a place again in the Dutch churches. The decisions of the Synod were accepted by Reformed churches elsewhere.

Number 64: *The Pilgrim's Progress*
John Bunyan (1628-1688), a Baptist preacher and writer, grew up in Bedford, England, joined the army as a teenager, and later became a tinker, the trade of his father. He married a pious believer who led him to Christ. After his baptism

he joined the Baptist church and began preaching. Since he had not received permission from the Established Church he was arrested and thrown into jail in 1660. His family fell into severe poverty during this time and he was rarely permitted to see them. Yet, despite these circumstances, he wrote one of the great classics of literature, *The Pilgrim's Progress*, while imprisoned. The Act of Pardon freed him in 1672 and he became pastor of the Bedford Baptist Church, a congregation he served until his death. He wrote other books including *The Holy War* and *Grace Abounding*.

Impact: His allegory *The Pilgrim's Progress* is considered one of the great works of Christian literature and was often one of only two books, along with the Bible, that families owned for over 200 years until the early twentieth century.

Number 65: The Westminster Assembly

The Westminster Assembly was one of the outstanding ecclesiastical gatherings in the long history of the Church. It was not limited in membership to the English, and its conclusions became the doctrinal basis of most dissenting bodies in England and America for two centuries. It was the crystallization of the Puritan movement in England since most of the Anglican clergy did not attend. The Assembly was regulated by Parliament, which took over the ecclesiastical functions of the king. The meetings were held in Westminster Abbey in the summer of 1643. The group proceeded to revise the Thirty-nine Articles, agreed unanimously on a Directory for Public Worship, and tackled the subject of church government. Five Congregationalists in the Assembly pressed their own opinions in favor of independency, but the majority made presbyterianism the form of government for the national Church. The Assembly completed its work by providing two catechisms. The Larger Catechism contained a full exposition of church doctrines and government while the Shorter Catechism omitted the subject of organization.

Impact: The most famous document from the Assembly was the Westminster Confession of Faith. It was strictly Calvinistic and as such not only met the needs of English Presbyterians, but it was adopted by the Church of Scotland to take the place of the Scottish creed of 1560. It became the basis of Congregationalist creeds, and it was the model for statements of doctrine by English and American Baptists.

Number 66: Congregationalists in the New World

In 1620 a group of Congregationalists built their first settlement in Plymouth, Massachusetts. Ten years later a second settlement started on Massachusetts Bay around Boston Harbor. The settlers were Puritans who were out of sympathy with the Church and State at home and who saw an opportunity for better fortunes in America. They were conformists in England, but the first church at Salem adopted the Congregational principle of limiting church membership to persons of spiritual qualification. The group affiliated itself with the Congregational Church at Plymouth. Other churches of the Massachusetts Colony followed the example of Salem with the result that two Congregational colonies were planted on the Massachusetts shore. Soon thousands more found their way to New England and settled in New Haven and at points along the Connecticut River. These were all outposts of Congregationalism, but Boston was its center. The Puritans wished only for the freedom to establish the kind of a church that had been unlawful at home. They were quick to take precautionary measures against the admission of any fanatical sects. In 1650 a colonial law was passed requiring the specific consent of the Government for the introduction of any other group than the adopted Congregational faith.

Impact: The English Government compelled the colonial Government to be more hospitable to persons who did not conform to colonial Congregationalism. In 1691 the original charter of the colony was taken away and a substitute provided. By that time Baptist and Episcopal churches had been founded in Boston.

Number 67: Baptists in the New World

In 1638 a few persons who had been members of a Congregational Church near London organized as a Baptist Church. They had the same principle as the church started by John Smyth at Amsterdam, except that they were Calvinistic in doctrine. The next year Roger Williams, who had been expelled from Massachusetts and had made a settlement at Providence on Narragansett Bay, organized a Baptist Church in his colony. Holding to the Congregational principle of spiritual qualification for church membership, but insisting on the same qualifications for baptism, they rejected infant baptism. Like the Anabaptists they carried the principle of personal religion to the point where they demanded religious liberty and the separation of Church and State. The mode of baptism was not an issue at first, but within a few years immersion was the universal custom. In polity the Baptists were congregational, but they organized associations of churches and even a general assembly among some of them in England, though these had little or no authority over the local churches. They depended on the Bible rather than on church creeds for their standards of doctrine, but to explain and clarify their beliefs they issued confessions of faith.

Impact: In 1707 American Baptists in Philadelphia organized their first association of churches, and other groups of Baptist churches followed their example. They were active in evangelism wherever they went. Through the Philadelphia Association the South was indoctrinated with Baptist ideas, though the Southern colonies were officially Anglican in religion.

Number 68: Quakers in the New World

Many Baptists in England were attracted to George Fox when he became a traveling preacher in about 1650. Fox championed an inner illumination of spirit, in contrast to the Congregationalists who stressed church membership and the Baptists who emphasized personal responsibility to God and the baptism of believers. Fox, though an uneducated man, believed that he had a message to give to the public. He preached the possibility of direct enlightenment through the influence of the Holy Spirit and the experience of God's love. In the face of war and hate he pleaded for peace and goodwill, and in the midst of an uncompromising Calvinism he proclaimed that God was striving to reconcile everyone to Himself. He gave the Bible less prominence than did most of the Dissenters, and he saw no need for sacraments or ordained ministers. The common people welcomed this unconventional kind of religion.

Impact: Within ten years about sixty preachers were imitating Fox. Few leaders of high standing joined them, except for William Penn, an admiral's son, who was able to plant a Quaker colony in America in 1681. From here the Quakers carried their message through the colonies. In parts of the South they were the most popular of the religious sects. Their idiosyncrasies, however, annoyed the Puritans of Boston so much that several persons were hung after a sentence of banishment had failed to dispose of them. In the Middle colonies they became one of the most respectable and prosperous elements in society.

Number 69: The Acts of Toleration

Since King Charles II had no deep religious convictions it suited him to be indulgent in religious matters. By 1672 he was ready to grant indulgence to Dissenters. The word "indulgence" implied permission to do something that in itself was wrong but that would not be punished. The word "toleration" likewise implied a grudging attitude and a power to grant or to withhold. It did not acknowledge a rightful claim, but only admitted a difference that would be overlooked. The idea of religious liberty to think and feel and do according to the dictates of the individual conscience was in harmony with the Renaissance conception of the worth of the person. But the Anabaptists and Quakers alone among the reformers believed that humanity's relation to God was so personal that no civil authority had any right to interfere. The Revolution of 1688, which drove James II from the throne, was accompanied by two constructive measures of legislation. One was the Bill of Rights, the other the Toleration Act – both passed by Parliament in 1689. The former forbade the king to make use of dispensations, to usurp the functions of the courts, to levy taxes, or to keep an army of his own. The right of the English people to make petition was also assured. The Toleration Act put limits on the authority of the Church. All groups were granted the right to their own independent worship, although the Church of England was recognized as the national church order. In America attempts by the Baptists to secure special privileges at the time of the renunciation of the English political allegiance were unsuccessful. It was not until 1833 that legislation was secured in Massachusetts that gave to all churches the same legal recognition.

Impact: The progress of democracy contributed to the on-going proliferation of different sects in America.

Number 70: The Enlightenment

Increasingly in the late seventeenth century and well into the eighteenth freedom of thought was producing skepticism both inside and outside of the churches. Most of the political leaders were distinctly irreligious. Many in the clergy were content to argue for a belief in God and the reasonableness of virtue without attempting to vindicate Christianity as a revealed religion. Known as the Enlightenment, this era was a time of new, secular philosophies. Medieval Schoolmen had tried to prove their faith by their reason but had failed and had fallen back on their traditional beliefs. The humanists of the Renaissance put a new valuation on intellectual powers but most stopped short of dismissing religion. By the seventeenth century, however, faith was being tossed out in favor of human reason. Humanistic philosophers emphasized a person's ability to win salvation without supernatural aid. They did not share the traditional Protestant opinion of human depravity and helplessness, nor did they recognize the need of atonement. They did not think of Christ as divine. Interest in scientific investigation was also spreading and philosophers were ready to argue for an inductive rather than a deductive method of reasoning. The new sciences with their reliance upon natural law were contrary to prevailing ideas in religion.

Impact: With philosophy and science both stressing humanity's power to discover truth by reason alone, it was easy to think of God as expressed in nature rather than in revelation. At best He was a creator with no active interest in His creation. Deism came to dominate the religious landscape in many affluent, intellectual, and legislative circles.

Number 71: Pietism

In Germany the evangelical movement of Pietism aroused people to a need for a power greater than themselves. It was also a reaction to the inertness and dogmatism of Lutheranism. Theological controversy in Germany had as its consequences an insistence on dogma, a popular indifference to religion, a neglect of instruction of the young people in the fundamentals of faith, and a low level of character and ideals among the clergy. The Thirty Years' War had demoralized the people as well as left the country barren and desolate. Philip Spener (1635-1705) of Frankfort was the first person of note among the Pietists. He saw the evil conditions of his times, took young men into his parsonage to prepare them practically for the ministry, and showed them how to deal with the unenlightened popular mind. As a pastor he tried to make his sermons intelligible to the uneducated, but he realized that he was not very successful and therefore invited his people to come together on a weekday evening, where he reviewed the Sunday lesson and explained any difficult points. Later at Dresden and Berlin he used similar methods and encouraged more lay participation in church activities. His book, *Pious Desires*, aroused opposition, but he revived the Lutheran religion. August Francke (1663-1727) succeeded Spener in the leadership of the Pietists. His chief work was done at Halle, where he was pastor and university teacher. The University of Halle became the center of the influence of Pietism. Francke lectured on the Bible, and revolutionized theological teaching elsewhere as well. Christian Schwartz and several other Pietists planted Christianity in India a hundred years before English Baptists sent William Carey to Calcutta.

Impact: Pietism did not create a new ecclesiastical organization, but remained as a force inside Lutheranism. It owed most of its impetus to Spener and Francke, but it was not confined to them alone. Nor was its force spent in Germany, for it made its way into Scandinavia and was welcomed in the cities of Switzerland. There it proved dynamic in awakening an interest in religion among university students and among the people of some of the larger cities. It lost ground because of the lack of leaders to follow Francke, and because of a growing wave of skepticism in Germany.

Number 72: The Moravian Brethren

Among the pupils of Francke at Halle was the heir to a large estate in Saxony. Impressed with the spirit of the place and deeply influenced by the missionaries whom he met, Count Zinzendorf became the moving spirit of the Moravian Brethren in the early part of the eighteenth century. When the Moravians, who had been widely persecuted for their pious convictions, did not know where to make a home, he welcomed them to his estate and became their friend and leader. Their settlement was called

Herrnhut, and here they lived on the simple principle of a common love for Christ. Zinzendorf held them together, preserved the ancient succession of bishops, and maintained worship. The life of the people was semimonastic for they lived in groups, wore a distinctive costume, and were governed as a congregation under the superintendency of Zinzendorf. In 1737 he was ordained bishop of the Moravian Church. Zinzendorf had the twofold purpose of spiritualizing the churches of Europe and undertaking to evangelize foreign lands. In pursuit of the former he traveled widely in northern Europe, and the brethren spread into a number of different countries. Schools were founded, partly for the education of children and partly for the training of Christian workers. The Moravians did not try to proselytize among the Protestants of Europe, but instead organized classes for Bible study and prayer, and to quicken and enrich the spiritual lives of the people.

Impact: The Moravians were never ambitious to become a great church, but in proportion to their numbers they surpassed all other Protestant bodies in foreign missions. At a time when missionary work was scarcely conceived by other Christian denominations, they were undertaking the most heroic tasks in such difficult countries as Greenland, Lapland, and the West Indies, though they had small resources and their missionaries were mostly untrained. The time came when they had more than twice as many members on their foreign mission fields as in their home churches. America proved an asylum for the Moravians, as it did for so many other religious refugees.

They mostly settled in Pennsylvania, where Zinzendorf visited and organized them with churches, schools, and industries.

Number 73: "Amazing Grace"

John Newton (1725-1807), the author of the hymn "Amazing Grace," was born in London, the son of a pious mother who died when he was only seven years of age. His only "schooling" was from his eighth to his tenth year. He was engaged in the African slave trade for several years, and was even himself held as a slave at one time in Sierra Leone. He bragged of his sinful nature, but was converted in a storm at sea while returning from Africa. He married a devout Christian in 1750 and became a minister in the Established Church in 1758, preaching at a church in Olney, near Cambridge. He remained here for nearly sixteen years, becoming friends with the poet William Cowper, who was joint author with him of the *Olney Hymns* in 1779. Soon after the appearance of this volume he moved to London where he was rector of St. Mary Woolnoth. Newton wrote his own epitaph, which included the following: John Newton, once an infidel and libertine, was, by the rich mercy of our Lord and Saviour Jesus Christ, preserved, restored, and pardoned, and appointed to preach the Faith he had long labored to destroy.

Impact: "Amazing Grace" is probably the most beloved song ever written and has had lasting influence on believers and nonbelievers alike to this day.

Number 74: The Great Awakening in America
Early in the eighteenth century in Northampton,
Massachusetts Jonathan Edwards served as pastor of the
most important church outside of Boston. Mystical in
temperament, sensitive to sin wherever he found it, and
distrusting the means of grace used by his predecessors,
he aroused his people with fear of future punishment for
their sins. The result was an emotional upheaval (c. 1735)
that brought large numbers of people to his church. From
Northampton revival spread down the river and along the
coast, primarily through the work of an Englishman who
had associated with the Wesley brothers at Oxford named
George Whitefield. Sailing to America in 1740, he landed
at Philadelphia and made preaching tours among the
colonies from New Hampshire to Georgia. Thousands were
drawn by his eloquence and many left their occupations at
a moment's notice when they heard of his coming, crowding
the buildings in which he spoke. Thirty thousand were said
to have gathered to hear him on Boston Common. He made
repeated journeys back and forth between England and
America, and proved a powerful religious force in both
countries. Tens of thousands of persons joined the churches,
and many became evangelistic ministers.
Impact: The Great Awakening on the whole set in motion
currents that affected deeply the future of American
Christianity. It revived personal religion, prompted the
Protestant missionary enterprise somewhat later, gave an
impetus to education, and kindled a new humanitarian spirit.

Number 75: New England Theology
In addition to sparking the Great Awakening, Jonathan Edwards was the founder of a school of theology that dominated the New England churches outside of the Boston area and the schools of religion for more than a century. Edwards was joined in his cause by Joseph Bellamy, a Yale graduate, and by Samuel Hopkins, his neighbor for many years in the Berkshire Hills of western Massachusetts. Bellamy broadened Edwards' theory of a limited atonement and Hopkins contributed the *System of Doctrines*, an exposition on Edwards' theology, and was considered a second founder of the New England theology. The ideas of these three men developed under the spur of practical need. As pastors they realized how the Old Calvinism had dulled the consciences of the people by the belief in the absolute impossibility of making the least approach to God. They tried to humanize the salvation experience without losing the main emphasis on the sovereignty of God. In the next generation Jonathan Edwards the Younger was driven to adopt a modified theory of the atonement because of the rise of the Universalists. Universalism had come to America from England with John Murray, a preacher who gained a wide following. Elhanan Winchester, converted from the Baptists of New England, was an equally popular preacher of a doctrine that all persons would be saved because Christ had entirely satisfied the demands of God's justice. To counteract the Universalists the Younger Edwards presented a governmental theory of the atonement similar to that of

Hugo Grotius, the Dutch Arminian, which vindicated the benevolence of God, but insisted that the atonement of Christ satisfied the "general" rather than the "distributive" justice of God. In other words Christ satisfied the demands of the moral law but that every person must meet the penalty of their own misdeeds.

Impact: The theory of the atonement of the junior Edwards became the accepted theory of the Congregational churches of New England, and thence spread to the Presbyterians and the Baptists

Number 76: The Rise of Wesleyanism

About the time of the Great Awakening in America two revivals broke out in Great Britain which profoundly affected the religious and social life of the people. One of these was in Wales where Griffith Jones was preaching in Carmarthenshire. Believing that people must be intelligent if they are to be good Christians, he founded circulating schools where thousands of children and adults learned to read the Welsh Bible. Other preachers also won many converts. In England there were pious folk among the laity and a few spiritually minded men like William Law among the clergy, but gambling, cock and bear fighting, profanity, and degrading theaters were among the weaknesses of the people. Drunkenness prevailed everywhere. John Wesley was born into this England in 1703. Educated at Oxford, he became scrupulous in religious practices, but without an experience of the love of God in his heart. As leader of a Holy Club of kindred spirits he cultivated his own piety and that of his friends, but gained little satisfaction. On a missionary journey to Georgia he fell in with certain Moravians who created in him a desire for greater joy and peace in religion, and in a London meeting of a religious society he "felt his heart strangely warmed." From that time his love for Christ burned so strongly that he felt compelled to preach salvation through the love of God in Christ to all who would listen. His burning zeal was unwelcome in most Anglican pulpits, and he had to face the question of his future, though he was an ordained clergyman in the Church of England. Seeking an outlet for his new spiritual energies, Wesley carried his religious message to the Cornish miners of southwest England, preaching in the open fields to thousands of them. Wesley was reluctant to separate from the Church of England in which he had been reared, as Luther found it hard to break with Catholicism. He had a genius for organization and by forming classes of a few persons each, with a leader who could guide the formation of Christian character in each class, he trained lay leaders and lay learners at the same time, but they all remained inside the Church of England. It was decades before Wesley ventured to ordain members of a Methodist clergy. In London he bought an old cannon foundry and fitted it up for headquarters. Methodism soon became a recognized religious and social movement.

Impact: Along with his brother Charles, the great hymnist whose music was a key attraction for many to the movement, Wesley did much to save England from the social convulsions that came later in France. Tens of thousands of persons became connected with the Methodist societies before John Wesley died. In America they began to grow rapidly from the time Methodism started. Methodism was revolutionary in its conception of religious principles. In the Church of England salvation was theoretically a spiritual process to be secured through worship and the sacraments of the Church. The evangelical preaching of Wesley called for a definite repentance of sin, a wrestling with God for forgiveness, and an experience of peace and assurance. Feeling and volition were stressed more than intellectual assent and conformity to ecclesiastical custom. Directly and indirectly the Methodists contributed to the missionary and humanitarian enterprises of the nineteenth century.

Number 77: The great eighteenth century hymnists
Two men from the eighteenth century have had more comprehensive influence on church music in the ensuing ages than any others, with the possible exception of Johann Sebastian Bach. They are Isaac Watts and Charles Wesley. Watts (1674-1748) is actually considered the father of English hymnody. Born in Southampton, England, he was a precocious child who learned to read almost as soon as he could speak and wrote verses while still a young boy. He was firmly attached to the principles of the Nonconformists, for which his father had suffered imprisonment, and was therefore compelled to decline the advantages of the great English universities, which at that

time received only Church of England students. He attended instead the Dissenting academy in London. In 1705 he published his first volume of poems, *Horae Lyricae*, which was widely praised. His *Hymns and Spiritual Songs* appeared in 1707; *Psalms*, in 1719; and *Divine Songs for Children*, in 1720. He became pastor of an Independent Church in London in 1702 but was so frail due to ill health that much of the time the work of the parish was done by an assistant. He was buried in Westminster Abbey. Wesley (1708-1788) has been called "the poet of Methodism." Born in Epworth, England in 1707 he was educated at Westminster School and Oxford University, where he took his degree in 1728. It was while a student at Christ Church College that Wesley and a few associates, by strict attention to duty and exemplary conduct, won for themselves the derisive epithet of "Methodists." He was ordained a priest in the Church of England in 1735, and that same year he sailed with his brother John as a missionary to Georgia. They soon returned to England. He was not converted, according to his own convictions, until Whitsunday, May 21, 1738. On that day he received a conscious knowledge of sins forgiven, and this event was the real beginning of his mission as the singer of Methodism. His hymns can generally be classified as hymns of Christian experience ("O for a Thousand Tongues to Sing"); invitation hymns ("Come, Sinners, to the Gospel Feast"); sanctification hymns ("O for a Heart to Praise My God"); funeral hymns ("Rejoice for a Brother Deceased"); and hymns on the love of God ("Wrestling Jacob"). He was not a singer alone, but as an itinerant preacher he was a busy and earnest co-laborer with his brother. After his marriage, in 1749, his itinerant labors were largely restricted to London and Bristol. Incredibly he wrote more than 6,500 hymns.

Impact: Their hymns have encouraged believers and spread the Gospel message for more than two centuries.

Number 78: Revival along the Appalachian frontier

Frontier religion in the late eighteenth century was marked by its emotionalism. This was due in part to a love of adventure among those who ventured beyond the relative safety of New England. When people moved farther away into the open country, new churches were seldom feasible at first. If they were to be given any religion it was through the willingness of ministers to travel endlessly, or through an organization that would supply religious instruction. Both methods were tried. Baptist pastors at times left their churches for a preaching tour. Others gave most of their time to an unattached mission as evangelists. Associations of churches appointed their agents to go into the South or to the western frontier of New York and Canada. Both Massachusetts and Connecticut Congregationalists organized voluntary missionary societies near the end of the eighteenth century. In 1801 a Plan of Union was arranged between Congregationalists and Presbyterians for missionary undertakings in the new West. Volunteer societies worked best because they were composed of only those persons who were interested and would contribute to the expenses. Missionaries sent out by such societies were paid meager salaries as contributions were small, but they worked faithfully in the midst of loneliness, fatigue, and numerous hardships. Outdoor gatherings, similar to those of Whitefield, attracted crowds of people. **Impact:** The opportunity for social gatherings had a powerful appeal to people who were starving for companionship. They were stirred by the evangelistic drive of the preachers, who encouraged emotional expression. The same exhibitions of tearful remorse and exuberant joy that appeared in England under Wesley's preaching and in the Great Awakening in America appeared on the frontier. Out of the conversions of the camp meetings the churches gathered recruits and the morals of the region showed dramatic improvement.

Number 79: Stages of revival in the American West
By the 1820s the expansion of settlers moving westward had increased dramatically. Once they had crossed the mountains it was comparatively easy to go on. Many built rafts and floated with the current down the Ohio River to the Mississippi; others penetrated the Lake country farther north into Canada. They pushed up tributary streams, avoiding the unbroken forests and made their way across Indiana and Illinois. The evangelization of the new West was not accomplished with a great deal of unity or planning. Missionaries went out to where the need seemed greatest. The country was so vast that administration was largely in the hands of the individual missionaries. There were four stages in the missionary march toward the West. The first

was in the lake and river country east of the Mississippi where close to a million had settled by 1835. The second was a ministry to the Native Americans on the prairies. After the Civil War many soldiers and other Americans settled on the prairie along with recent European immigrants. These groups, along with Indians that had unfairly and cruelly been forced onto reservations, were touched by the Gospel message brought by earnest and devoted missionaries. The third stage carried the missionaries to the open ranges and the mountains where ranchers, cowboys, and miners constituted a rough and somewhat lawless element. The fourth stage to the Pacific had already been reached before the country was much settled.

Impact: Without the tireless efforts of Christian missionaries, the young nation would have had no moral compass and many of the important social programs that helped protect immigrants, women, children, Native Americans, and newly freed slaves would have never existed.

Number 80: Missions to the Native Americans

When the Europeans came to the New World they felt it was their responsibility to convert the natives and soon both Catholics and Protestants were at work among them, each in their own way. Friars were commissioned to accompany the Spanish exploring expeditions, and by the time the Puritans were busy with their Massachusetts Bay settlements over forty Catholic missions had been established in Florida with nearly thirty thousand adherents. During the same period Franciscan missionaries went into the Southwest with Spanish expeditions and rapidly won the Indians to the Catholic religion. French missionaries went further than the Spaniards. The Jesuits made perilous journeys among unknown lakes and streams and through the forests. From Maine up through the St. Lawrence valley, westward along the Great Lakes, and down the upper tributaries of the Mississippi the missionaries paddled their canoes, searching out native villages. Sometimes they suffered terrible torture and martyrdom, but they persisted resolutely in their purpose. They planted the cross where they preached, baptized their converts, and administered the sacrament of the mass. In Louisiana French Catholicism gained a permanent foothold, but after the English conquest there was little to show for their pioneering in the Mississippi valley. Although most English colonists were hostile to the natives, attempts were made by many dedicated believers to share Protestant Christianity. An early colonial law required the instruction of Indian children in Virginia, and William and Mary College made provision for the education of Indian youth. Roger Williams made friends among the natives and prepared a *Key to the Indian Language.* The Quakers and the Moravians went among the Indians of the Iroquois Confederacy, and David Brainerd, by his brief but singularly devoted life, gained fame for his efforts to win the Delaware Indians. In 1810 the Congregationalists of the United States organized the first foreign missionary society and promptly sent missionaries to the Indians of Georgia.

Impact: Sadly the Indians came to be regarded as wards of the Government, and it became national policy to place them on specified reservations. The missionaries sent out by Eastern societies were the only groups sympathetic to this maltreatment and they tried to help by building schools, churches, and clinics.

Number 81: The introduction of existential philosophy

Soren Aaby Kierkegaard (1813-1855) was born in Copenhagen, Denmark and exhibited from an early age the depression and insecurity that would plague him his entire life. He studied theology at the University of Copenhagen, graduating in 1840, but was never ordained. Most of his life was spent writing existential works that stressed the necessity of a moral life and the "otherness" of God. His best known work, *Either-Or*, was an anonymously published debate between ethical and aesthetic ideas. In his last years he wrote works that argued against the theology and practice of the Danish state church on the grounds that religion is for the individual soul and is to be separated absolutely from the state and the world.

Impact: Kierkegaard's exisential writings greatly influenced the Neo-orthodox theologians of the early twentieth century.

Number 82: The Moody crusades

In 1870 Dwight L. Moody, an American evangelist and Sunday school worker, stirred the people of Great Britain by religious campaigns in the large halls of the provincial cities of England and Scotland, and then in London where for months he attracted crowds to his meetings. He preached the evangelical gospel of human sin and the necessity of salvation through Jesus Christ, but he also emphasized the love of God that sought to draw the sinner to Himself. Moody was able to recover many who had lost interest in religion and he aroused thousands of unchurched people. He returned to America and for a number of years he continued his successful career of evangelism, supplementing it with the development of educational institutions which he organized for boys and girls. In his later years he held summer conferences at Northfield, Massachusetts that drew together thousands of Christian people eager to hear the best speakers and leaders from England and America. Although not formally trained, Moody was a gifted speaker and evangelist and by 1871 he had erected a large church on LaSalle Street, near the site of the current Moody Memorial Church. Ira David Sankey joined him in Chicago and helped him further his evangelistic efforts with hymn singing. An advocate of education, Moody opened the Northfield seminary for young women in 1879 in Northfield, Massachusetts and, in 1881, the adjacent Mount Hermon School for boys. In 1889 he established in Chicago the first Bible school of its kind in the country, the Chicago Evangelization Society.

Renamed later the Moody Bible Institute, it trained Christian workers in Bible study and in practical methods of social reform. He founded the Colportage Association in 1895 to produce Christian literature at a modest price for mass distribution. He died during a crusade in Kansas City.

Impact: In addition to the many programs and institutions Moody established and the countless people he led to Christ, he and Sankey created a model for teamwork that influenced future evangelists like Billy Sunday and Billy Graham.

Number 83: The Salvation Army

The Salvation Army began in 1865 as an evangelizing agency to reach those who lived in the dreadful British city slums, which at that time had no churches. William and Catherine Booth, a Methodist couple, started an independent ministry in the heart of London. They pitched their gospel tent in the slums and won over many despite the taunts of most of the locals. In 1878 William introduced military features into his organization, which was already growing beyond England. As general of the Salvation Army he continued to direct its policies with autocratic power, establishing posts in various cities of England, North America, the European Continent, and Asia. With unique methods, including band music, people were drawn to open-air meetings on street corners and in halls, and were told to give up their sinful lives. Again and again men and women were rescued from the depths of despair and were transformed by the power of Christ's love. The Army later broadened its work to include social services because of the great needs of the people among whom it ministered. After 1889 the Army established rescue homes, farm colonies, and labor bureaus. Booth obtained money for his enterprises from the sale of his best-selling book, *In Darkest England and the Way Out*, and from wealthy friends of the movement.

Impact: Catherine died of cancer but not before she had worked tirelessly to secure the passage of laws that improved the lives of women and children. William lived another two decades and saw his organization spread to 55 countries. During his lifetime he traveled over five million miles and preached about 60,000 sermons. The Salvation Army continues to thrive and provide help for those in need, in Christ's name, throughout the world.

Number 84: The German Inner Mission

With the decline of Pietism and the rising strength of rationalism German religion in the early nineteenth century seemed formal and unreal. The people needed to be stirred to an increased interest in a vital, practical religion. Several groups and individuals rose to meet the challenge. For instance, the Evangelical Union of Lutherans and Calvinists, formed in 1817 in Prussia and several other states, was an organization of Bible and tract societies dedicated to the distribution of religious literature. And John Frederick Oberlin worked tirelessly to bring the Gospel to the country folk of the Alsatian Mountains. Of particular note was John H. Wichern who founded the Inner Mission in Hamburg that was designed to meet the physical and spiritual needs of the poor. Along with Theodore Fliedner, the Inner Mission's second great leader, Wichern's work spread throughout central Europe. Fliedner, an organizational genius, developed deaconess associations, which established so-called "motherhouses," including hospitals, orphanages, and rescue homes, and enrolled thousands of women for Christian service. Relocating their center to Kaiserswerth, the Inner Mission sent foreign missionaries to many countries to undertake similar service. Stimulated by the evangelistic meetings held in England and America, both ministers and lay preachers evangelized among the people, holding special tent and theater meetings.

Impact: The Inner Mission enlarged its scope beyond the expectations of its founders. Various organizations were created for children and young adults. Numerous agencies were established to cope with social ills. In short, it served a vital ministry role during the nineteenth century.

Number 85: English and Scottish foreign missions

William Carey, called "the father of modern missions," was born in Paulersbury, England to a poor weaver. As a young man he worked as an apprentice to a shoemaker but spent his spare time studying for the ministry. Amazingly, while still a teenager, he was able to read the Bible in six languages. This gift for language would serve him well as a missionary. In 1787 he became pastor of a Baptist church where, in 1792, he preached a sermon with the famous line, "Expect Great Things from God, Attempt Great Things for God." He helped organize the Baptist Missionary Society and became one of the group's first members to go abroad when he went to India in 1793. He suffered greatly during the early years of his ministry due to financial setbacks, the death of his children, and the mental illness of his wife. In 1799 he was able to purchase a small indigo plantation and it was from here that he started his first successful mission. Opposition from the East India Company forced him to shut down his operation, however, so in 1800 he moved to Serampore where he and other missionaries preached, taught, and started Serampore Press to distribute Christian literature. In 1831 Carey was appointed professor of Oriental languages at Fort William College in Calcutta, a position he held for 30 years until his death. During this time he was largely responsible for translating the Bible into 36 dialects, making the Scriptures available to over 300 million people. In addition to Carey, the London Missionary Society sent its first missionaries into the islands of the Pacific Ocean, where they had remarkable success among the islanders, though they had to contend with cruel and greedy traders and sailors. The Wesleyan Missionary Society brought Christianity to the Pacific islands, Africa, and the Far East. The Scotch Presbyterians sent out pioneer missionaries to West Africa as early as 1796. Both the Established Church and the Free Church organized foreign mission committees. Among well-known Scotch missionaries were Alexander Duff, who established Presbyterian schools in India; John Paton, who spent the bulk of his life working in the New Hebrides;

Robert Moffat, who started a mission station in South Africa in about 1820; and David Livingstone, who explored the Zambesi and the great lakes of the interior and who helped to destroy the African slave trade in the mid-nineteenth century.

Impact: English and Scottish missions in the late eighteenth and early to mid-nineteenth centuries not only brought the Gospel message, they were also instrumental in fomenting social reforms, bringing medical care, and ending pagan practices that destroyed the lives of women and children.

Number 86: American foreign missions

The missionary undertakings in Great Britain attracted the attention of Americans, and soon they were contributing to the expenses of the English stations. Yet it wasn't until the nineteenth century that any national foreign society was organized. A group of Williams College students in 1806 formed the Haystack Band of volunteers. This group helped form the American Board of Commissioners for Foreign Missions, officially organized by the Congregationalists in 1810. Adoniram Judson and Luther Rice were the first missionaries sent by this society, sailing to India in 1812; although Judson and Rice soon transferred their allegiance to the Baptists over a dispute over baptism with their mission board. Judson and his wife Anne moved to Burma where they lived in the English Baptist mission home. He began an earnest study of the Burmese language, although it took him nearly six years to gain the necessary linguistic skills to preach in the native tongue. It was another six years before he led the first person to Christ. In 1824 the Anglo-Burmese war broke out and Judson was imprisoned for two years. Shortly after his release Anne died. Judson continued his work and in 1833 he completed a translation of the Bible into Burmese. During this time he married Sarah Hall Boardman, returning to America in 1845 due to her failing health. Sadly she died on the voyage. He went back to Burma in 1846 and spent the rest of his life working on a Burmese dictionary. Like his second wife, he also died at sea while sailing to Martinique where he hoped to recuperate from an illness.

Impact: For nearly thirty years Presbyterians and other Reformed churches contributed to the American Board, but at the end of that period denominational organization seemed to each group a better arrangement. Both Methodists and Episcopalians followed the example of the rest. Smaller denominations carried on independent operations in various regions.

Number 87: The rise of the Sunday school movement
In 1824 the American Sunday School Union was organized to extend Sunday schools throughout the country and to provide religious resources. Within five years it had issued more than six million copies of Sunday school publications. In the first decade of the twentieth century it organized thousands of new schools, resulting in hundreds of churches. The various denominations promptly organized for educational purposes, establishing their publishing houses for the issue of tracts and books, and providing printed

helps for Bible study. The earliest method of studying the Bible was to memorize parts of Scripture, and question books were prepared for drills in knowledge of the Bible. The American Sunday School Union introduced a plan for a five year course of Bible study, with select verses, questions, and notes for every Sunday. In 1865 the plan of a lesson quarterly was adopted by the Sunday School Union, which became very popular. Sunday school institutes and conventions helped to stimulate interest and to invent improvements. At one such convention a lesson committee of Sunday school publishers was appointed to prepare lessons to cover the entire Bible in seven years. For decades the Sunday schools of the evangelical churches in America and Britain used this uniform lesson system. Naturally the denominational publishing houses with their valuable plates and copyrights did not want to make many changes to the lessons. But dissatisfaction grew as the lessons did not seem suited for small children, grading was not provided for, and adult instruction was inadequate. Attempts to provide better methods and lesson helps were made independently.

Impact: The steady improvement of secular schools made it imperative that Sunday schools should be improved if they were to truly help their pupils, and by the end of the nineteenth century it was evident that extensive modifications must be made. A particularly valuable experiment was the instruction of teachers at summer assemblies and by means of local study classes. The Chautauqua Movement for popular education grew out of a summer assembly for the better training of Sunday school teachers. It outlined a system of reading courses that were adopted widely by local groups of teachers and other interested persons, with an annual gathering at Chautauqua, New York. These assemblies lasted for several weeks with lectures and intensive study. In 1903 the Religious Education Association was organized to put religious education on a broader basis than the Sunday school. Composed mainly of ministers and educators, it was organized into expert commissions which investigated conditions, planned improvements, and published useful aids for religious education. This group was not only active in the Sunday schools but they also worked with colleges, Young Men's Christian Associations, and young people's societies.

Number 88: The Oxford movement

In about 1820 at Oxford University Thomas Arnold, in an effort to address the problem of declining church attendance, advanced the idea of including in one national Church all Christians except Unitarians and Catholics. Edward B. Pusey, R. H. Froude, and John Henry Newman, on the other hand, believed that the best way to arouse a new interest in the faith was to issue tracts on ecclesiastical subjects. Their proposed association was short-lived, but the *Tracts for the Times*, which gave the Oxford men the name of Tractarians, proved valuable as a means of instructing the people in the principles of the Church. Newman was the principal writer of the *Tracts*. He had a clear and simple style that influenced many. Eventually he abandoned his Calvinistic heritage and embraced Roman Catholicism. His *Apologia* explained his conviction that "outside the Catholic Church all things tend to atheism." In an adaptation of the prevalent evolutionary teachings he tried to justify his adherence to Rome by showing that Catholicism was a development of primitive Christianity. Newman was not the only Protestant scholar who went over to Rome at this time, but he was the most conspicuous. The other members of the Oxford group maintained a middle ground between Catholicism and Protestantism. After Newman's defection Edward Pusey became the head of the Oxford movement.

Impact: The Oxford movement resulted in a new impetus toward old customs. It gave momentum to a Catholic trend in the Church of England, which made the High Church party a growing force in the religious life and social activity of Great Britain.

Number 89: The rise of denominational seminaries
In America the first colleges were intended primarily for theological students. By the nineteenth century, however, it was becoming clear that special schools should be provided for ministerial candidates. Soon various denominations had standardized the theological curriculum in a three-year course of post-college seminary instruction. The programs were based chiefly on the literature of the Bible, systematic theology and apologetics, practical courses in homiletics and pastoral methods, lectures on church

history, and the art of public speaking. Certain denominations like the Presbyterians were insistent on an educated ministry; others like the Methodists did not make such demands generally, only among those who ministered to large, prominent congregations. With the broadening of general culture and the introduction of new subjects into the college curriculum the theological schools were compelled to improve their facilities. Instead of taking ministers from the pulpit to fill chairs of instruction, schools turned more and more to the trained experts. Professors introduced new courses into the curriculum, including the social sciences, philosophy, and religious literature. A few students who wished to specialize went to England or Germany to acquaint themselves first hand with European scholarship. In addition, with the increase of evangelism and the multiplication of opportunities for service in the churches there was a growing demand for religious workers other than ministers in both the home churches and in mission countries. To meet these demands training schools were founded, like Moody Bible Institute in Chicago, which gave a less thorough preparation, but which provided students with something of the technique of religious work. **Impact:** From seminaries and Bible schools went thousands of young men and women eager for Christian work, ministering and serving wherever the opportunities opened.

Number 90: Social reform in Britain
While the French Revolution called attention to social misery in other countries besides France, it was in England

and America that the humanitarian spirit found its greatest opportunity to breathe. Christians who were conscious of social wrongs gave particular attention in England to poverty, intemperance, slavery, and industrial ills. Methodism had carried religion to the working people. Wesley had tried outreach experiments and had been active in philanthropy. But agricultural conditions kept the rural people poor and the lack of schools kept them ignorant. The Industrial Revolution altered working conditions and enslaved the young and old alike. Those who couldn't pay their debts were commonly punished by imprisonment. Slavery in the British Empire was a national disgrace. These and other conditions aroused the Christian reformers. John Howard worked tirelessly to improve prison conditions. When he had secured better prison conditions in England he went to the European Continent where he died as a result of his persistent efforts. William Wilberforce secured the abolition of slavery throughout the Empire. And Lord Shaftesbury spent his career working for a number of reforms.

Impact: These and other men and women, among the first to be called evangelicals, organized the Church Missionary Society and other Bible and tract societies. Together they took the lead in social reform and helped to make significant and lasting changes in Britain, changes that inspired other believers around the world.

Number 91: Social reform in America

Humanitarianism took two forms in America in the nineteenth century: the improvement of lives through relief measures and attempt to eradicate the roots of social evils. Groups like the Quakers were especially sensitive to suffering and injustice. Others, unfortunately, did not see a need to end evils like slavery, cruel methods of punishment for criminals, or the life sentences given to debtors. Quakers took the lead in reform in Pennsylvania, and obtained a better legal code from the state legislature. Other states soon adopted improvements. Religion was carried into the prisons and methods of education were introduced. The Volunteers of America and the American Prison Association were also Christian agencies engaged in prison reform. Lyman Beecher of Connecticut and other ministers preached against alcohol abuse while the Woman's Christian Temperance Union, founded in 1874, helped form a Prohibition political party. The greatest evil of the age, though, was slavery. Entrenched in the South after the cotton industry became profitable, it became the defining issue of the nineteenth century. Slowly church people in the North came to believe that they could no longer cooperate with slaveholders, and the denominational organizations of Methodists, Baptists, and Presbyterians split apart. When Harriet Beecher Stowe's *Uncle Tom's Cabin* became a sensation, its story depicting the horrors of slavery fully awoke the Northern churches to the necessity of abolition. When the Civil War began in 1861 it was not only a war for the preservation of the Union against the secession of the slaveholding states, it was also a crusade for the emancipation of the slaves. Churches provided chaplains for the armies on both sides. The end came with a victory for the Union and the enforcement of the Emancipation Proclamation, which President Abraham Lincoln had issued in 1863.

Impact: While some reform efforts were successful, others failed over time. The net result to the churches, however, was an increased fervor to apply the Christian message of hope to every aspect of life.

Number 92: Papal infallibility

In 1864 Pope Pius IX, a man who had fallen out of favor and had fled Italy due to his meddling in national affairs, returned from exile and wrote *Syllabus of Errors*, a work devoted to condemning certain liberalizing social trends and claiming that the Church should have control over all secular affairs in the Papal States. At the Vatican Council in 1870 he established the dogma of Papal infallibility.

Impact: Along with his 1854 dogma of the Immaculate Conception, his rule on Papal infallibility remains as a dogma of the Catholic Church. Pius, however, retired as a prisoner to the Vatican after he refused to accept the abolishment of Vatican rule over the Papal States, which were made part of Italy. He died in prison.

Number 93: Christian Socialism

Influenced by the class struggle theories of Karl Marx, ministers like John Frederick Maurice of London and Charles Kingsley, a country rector, combined liberal theology with enough socialist doctrine to give them the name of Christian Socialists. They sympathized with the Chartist movement, which was intended to extend the privileges of the Reform Bill of 1832 to the working people, though Maurice and Kingsley could not go the full length of the Chartist demands. They accomplished little permanently, but they showed that there were leaders in the Church who took to heart the needs of the working classes. Maurice and Kingsley were successors of the evangelicals in their social mood and representatives of a Broad Church phase of Anglicanism, which was characterized by liberal thinking as well as social sympathy. Others, both Anglicans and Dissenters, who would not actually call themselves socialists, were still friendly to those who were struggling for social recognition and a better living. Robert Hall, an eminent Baptist preacher, championed the cause of the trade unions when they were unpopular. John Bright, a religious Independent, worked to give working people the right to vote. The Primitive Methodists, who separated from the parent body in 1808, found their opportunity for service among the miners, the factory workers, and the fishermen. Members of the High Church party of Anglican clergy organized the Guild of St. Matthew in 1877 and a Christian Social Union in 1889. These organizations had political, educational, and religious features, but they were designed particularly for the study of social problems and their solutions.

Impact: Each of these movements and efforts demonstrated the growing attitude among Protestants that the emphasis on individual salvation should not obscure the Church's social obligations.

Number 94: The impact of Charles Darwin

Almost simultaneously Charles Darwin and Alfred Russell Wallace announced a hypothesis on the process of natural evolution. Darwin stated in the *Origin of Species*, published in 1859, that all forms of life are related, that the origin of separate species came about by variations from an original type which Nature selected and perpetuated, and that the maintenance of life was possible only by the constant struggle for existence and the destruction of that which was not fitted to survive existing conditions. Darwin soon followed his first book with a second entitled the *Descent of Man*, in which he traced the genealogy of humankind from single-celled organisms by the same process of evolution. Many scientists accepted the interpretations of Darwin, but to the majority of Christians the whole idea of a process that made no provision for the directing hand of the Creator (at least for no further participation in the process after starting it in motion) was quite unsatisfactory. A struggle for existence, which destroyed multitudes and left those who were best fitted to survive, seemed far from Christian. A particularly unfortunate consequence of Darwin's doctrine of the struggle for existence and the survival of the strongest was the application of the idea of social evolution and a justification of the use of such evil acts as genocide and other atrocities. Philosophers like Nietzsche were aggressive champions of this theory. Similarly it was easy to justify ruthless competition in business in the same way. Progress seemed to mean the victory of the person, group, or nation with the most relentless drive. Soon apologists for a more generous philosophy arose. Henry Drummond, professor in the Free Church College in Glasgow, elaborated in his book *The Ascent of Man* the importance of individuals striving on behalf of others and offering themselves vicariously to help amend society's ills. For other Christian thinkers, though, evolution was seen as the instrument through which God works.

Impact: Ultimately there has been very little middle ground between those who hold a literal interpretation of Scripture and those who don't. As a result the impact of Darwin's views have continued to the present day.

Number 95: The application of Biblical criticism

Scientific methodology, which changed the understanding of natural processes, was soon applied to other areas of learning in the nineteenth century. Theologians, specifically, began employing the same principles of investigation to certain accepted convictions to try and arrive at conclusions that were based on evidence rather than on tradition, the authority of the church, or the Bible. The principles of historical criticism which were worked out and applied to religious as well as secular history were that human events occur in the midst of a specific physical and social environment and any institution, even the Church, must be studied as a product of that environment. Historical criticism had its home in Germany. It was the outgrowth of German rationalism, which appeared as an intellectual movement in the universities where the clergy were trained and then in church circles. The German rationalists took pride in their enlightenment and their intellectual processes. They embraced a natural religion, as did the English deists, but they deemed a religion of revelation unnecessary and unreliable. Every miracle and every mystery was subjected to rational thought. Critics tried fitting Scripture into the environment in which it was born.

Impact: What happened, naturally, was that interpretations that did not fit into preconceived notions were deemed "unscientific" and were discarded. Some declared that most of the Bible was not intended for all periods of time. Others tried to show that basic morality was superior to a religion of revelation. Eventually Genesis and certain New Testament writings were discarded, the miracles and the atonement were denied, Jesus Christ was declared nothing more than a man, and the Bible was simply a product of human minds. In Germany, and later in other parts of the world, sermons became essays on moral or civic duty. Christianity was taken out of the schools and the name of Christ from the hymnbooks. The *Life of Jesus* by David Strauss, published in 1835, took the position that the narratives of the Gospels were mythical and that the story of Jesus was mainly a product of the imagination. Other lives of Jesus continued to come from the presses of Germany, most of them critical of accepted dogma. By degrees the conclusions of these men became recognized by most of the leading scholars of English and American theological circles, although they were strenuously opposed by conservatives and only slowly filtered through to the lay mind.

Number 96: The rise of Liberalism

Another similar movement arose in the nineteenth century that attempted to knock down the walls of traditional Christianity. Friedrich Schleiermacher (1768-1834) tried to make the Christian faith acceptable to those who had been influenced by Enlightenment thinking. For this he is considered the father of "Liberal" theology, so called because he believed that the individual should be able to determine truth without the interference of any outside authority. Heavily influenced by German Romanticism, his writings paved the way for Enlightenment thinking to enter the Church. Among his teachings was the idea that each person has a God-consciousness that gives them a sense that something exists beyond the self and upon which each person is fully dependent. He held that Jesus was not God, he was simply a person who had fully achieved God-consciousness.

Impact: Liberal theology continues to have a great influence on the Christian church.

Number 97: The Metropolitan Tabernacle

Charles Haddon Spurgeon (1834-1892) was born in London, the son of a Congregational minister. He joined the Baptist church in 1850 after his conversion and began preaching immediately. Demonstrating powerful skills as an orator he filled the small chapels he spoke in to capacity. In the 1850s, while a vast new church was being built for him, he preached to audiences approaching 10,000 people at the Surrey Music Hall. When the Metropolitan Tabernacle was completed in 1861 it held over 6,000 and could be used for numerous church related and mission outreach functions, a new concept in that day. Among his many accomplishments was the creation of a monthly magazine, *The Sword and Trowel*; the publication of over 2,000 sermons and numerous books, including *Commenting and Commentaries*; the establishment of the Stockwell Orphanage, which housed 500 children; the creation of the Colportage Society to distribute books, tracts, and Bibles; and the establishment of a pastor's college.

Impact: Spurgeon and the Metropolitan Tabernacle are synonymous with nineteenth century evangelicalism and his paraphrased writings continue to sell widely.

Number 98: The Eastern churches

The nineteenth century was a great period of growth for the Orthodox churches in Russia and eastern Europe. As different nation states emerged from the former Ottoman Empire, national churches began to form. Among these churches were ones founded in Greece in 1833, Romania in 1864, Bulgaria in 1871, and Serbia in 1879. While the churches remained loyal to the patriarch of Constantinople, they became increasingly identified with their country. This was especially true in Russia where the church was virtually controlled by the state.

Impact: The church survived in spite of state interference in the nineteenth and twentieth centuries in large part because the peasant classes were devoted to the traditions of the faith, great writers like Tolstoy and Dostoevsky advanced the need for salvation in their works, and dedicated ministers quietly served unofficial flocks.

Number 99: The Student Volunteer movement

In 1886 Dwight L. Moody invited a group of college students to the Mt. Hermon conference grounds in Northfield, Massuchesetts for a month of Bible study and teaching. Of the 151 students who attended 21 agreed to pray together for the mission needs of the world. After about two weeks a preacher named A. T. Pierson spoke to the group about foreign missions. He was followed by speakers from different countries who detailed the spiritual needs among their people. After the conference core members of the group, led by Robert Wilder, went to colleges around the country and shared the excitement they had felt at Mt. Hermon. They asked other student to join them. By the end of the following year over 2,000 students had pledged their lives to missions. Led by John R. Mott and called the Student Volunteer Movement, the group's motto was "The evangelization of the world in this generation."

Impact: By 1915 over 5,000 missionaries had been sent to the field through the efforts of the Student Volunteer

Movement. Mott was also instrumental in creating other outreach organizations like the World's Student Christian Federation and the Laymen's Missionary Movement.

Number: 100: The rise of Protestant denominations
By the opening of the twentieth century Protestantism was represented by many denominations, both large and small. Most had broken off one of the major groups, which included the Anglicans, the Baptists, the Congregationalists, the Methodists, the Presbyterians, and the Lutherans.
Impact: As time went by sectarian differences became less important and denominations cooperated for such causes as evangelism, social action, and missionary activities.

Number 101: World War I
While national interests related to territorial rights, centuries old hatreds, and economic issues caused World War I, Christian leaders typically affirmed their national identities and declared the cause of their country alone to be holy. By the end of the war, however, many churches lay in ruins and, with over ten million people killed, a spiritual malaise hung over Europe.
Impact: Into this spiritual vacuum such secular philosophies as atheism, Marxism, and fascism gained prominence.

Number 102: Christian Pacifist movement
Highly unpopular during World War I, the Christian Pacifist movement nonetheless survived and was more readily

embraced when the War's terrible toll was realized. In World War II and the Korean War many pacifists went to battle in non-combat roles, like medics; actions that earned them grudging respect.

Impact: Because of their pioneering peace efforts, Christian pacifists gained great influence in the 1960s and 1970s during the Vietnam War.

Number 103: Pentecostal revival

In 1906 in an abandoned Methodist church on Azusa Street in Los Angeles a Pentecostal revival broke out that would eventually sweep the nation and have far-reaching influence around the world. Interestingly, during this time when racism was an ugly fact of daily life, an African-American preacher named William J. Seymour sparked the revival. Lasting for three years it became an international sensation.

Impact: The Azusa Street revival led to one of the most powerful Christian movements in the twentieth century.

Number 104: The Russian Revolution

World War I was especially destructive to the Russian economy, destroying cities and leaving the people in hopeless poverty. This situation did much to cause the Russian Revolution of 1917. Inspired by the writings of Karl Marx and Friedrich Engels and led by Vladimir Lenin, the Communist revolution was especially destructive to the Russian Orthodox churches since it was feared that the

Church was the one institution that could divide the loyalties of the people.

Impact: Within a few years Communist leaders had executed over 1,000 bishops and priests, had razed hundreds of ancient monasteries, and seized the church's treasuries and property. Yet totalitarianism could not ultimately extinguish the spirit of the people. After the fall of the Iron Curtain the Orthodox church thrived again.

Number 105: The first Christian radio broadcast

In 1920 the first radio station in the country, KDKA in Pittsburgh, began broadcasting. One of the station's engineers was a member of a local Episcopal church. Since the station needed programming it agreed to air the church's Sunday services. The response from listeners was so positive that fledgling stations around the country made church services an integral part of their weekly programming.

Impact: From these humble beginnings, religious broadcasting became a multi-billion dollar industry by the end of the century.

Number 106: The rise of Neo-orthodoxy

Karl Barth (1886-1968), a Swiss theologian, was the founder of the neo-orthodox school of theology. He studied at various universities in Germany and became a liberal pastor for twelve years in Switzerland. After seeing first hand the inherent sinfulness of humanity during World War I he began studying Scripture and theologians like Calvin and Kierkegaard. Eventually he abandoned liberal theology. In his multi-volume *Church Dogmatics* he detailed his beliefs, which included the ideas that God is transcendent and that humanity is separated from God due to sin – a condition that can only be resolved when the Holy Spirit reconciles us to God through Christ.

Impact: Neo-orthodox theology was, in many ways, universalist but was much more Christ-centered than the liberalism that reigned among scholars during the late nineteenth and early twentieth centuries.

Number 107: The Summer Institute of Linguistics

In 1917 Cameron Townsend was a young missionary in Guatemala, working among the Cakchiquel Indians. He had trouble learning their difficult language but by 1931 he had completed a full translation of the New Testament. When ill health forced Townsend and his wife back to the United States they decided to start a summer school to show missionaries how to translate the Scriptures into the many unwritten languages around the world. Called the Summer Institute of Linguistics, it began on a farm in Sulphur Springs, Arkansas in 1934. By the 1940s the Institute had grown to the point it required more than part time staff and temporary facilities. Renamed the Wycliffe Bible Translators in 1942, it became the world's leading translation ministry.

Impact: Today Wycliffe has nearly 6,500 workers in over 50 countries. Their efforts have produced Scripture portions in hundreds of languages.

Number 108: The rise of Fundamentalism

As the twentieth century opened modernism seemed to have established a firm grip on many of the denominations and most of the seminaries. Against this tide, Gresham Machen (1881-1937) stood as the intellectual center of conservative Christianity. Born in Baltimore, Machen was a tremendous scholar who studied at Johns Hopkins and Princeton in the United States and at Marburg in Germany. Ordained in 1914 he became a professor of New Testament literature at Princeton Theological Seminary. He left the school due to his conservative theology and the school's rapid drift toward liberalism. In 1929 he founded the Westminster Theological Seminary and became its president and professor of New Testament. He took similar steps when he resigned from the Presbyterian Board of Missions to found an independent society and when he and a group of like-minded clergy started the Orthodox Presbyterian church. On a popular front, the Fundamentalist movement was aided by the publication of The Fundamentals, a series of books financed by the president of the Union Oil Company, Lyman Stewart. The Fundamentals covered many doctrinal issues and were written by leading conservative preachers. Within six years nearly three million copies had been distributed.

Impact: For nearly 60 years, between the mid-1920s and the 1980s, Fundamentalism was a separatist movement that had little public influence. This changed when preachers like Pat Robertson and Jerry Falwell took up the mantle of past leaders and began stressing the need for national repentance and a return to conservative values.

Number 109: World War II

Peace treaties signed at the end of World War I did little to pacify the German people over various nationalistic issues and their concern about the spread of Communism. This dissatisfaction gave impetus to Adolph Hitler's fascist movement. While, sadly, most Protestant and Catholic groups chose not to defy Hitler, those that did were quickly eliminated or repressed. When Germany invaded Poland in 1939 World War II was officially launched. This was also the initiation of one of the greatest horrors in the history of humankind, the Jewish Holocaust. Hitler's rabid hatred of the Jews extended to Christians who he called "inventions" of Judaism.

Impact: After the war, with churches lying in ruin and many Christian leaders killed, Germany became very secular. In fact Europe, the cradle of the Reformation, is today the least religious continent in the world.

Number 110: The cost of discipleship

More Christians have been martyred in the last 100 years than during the previous 19 centuries. In Third World countries, Islamic kingdoms, and Communist nations Christians have been killed by the millions. After World War I, for instance, over one million Armenian Christians were exterminated by the Turks. Today, in countries like Sudan, Muslim insurgents kill, enslave, and rape Christians almost at will. One of the most famous twentieth century martyrs was Dietrich Bonhoeffer who fought for religious freedom in Nazi Germany. He was imprisoned and executed in 1945 as the war was coming to a close.

Impact: The early church leader Tertullian wrote during the Roman persecutions that "the blood of the martyrs is the seed of the Church." What was true then is true today as the worldly sacrifice of brave Christians serves to inspire others to take their place and continue preaching the Gospel message.

Number 111: The World Council of Churches

In 1910 a gathering of 1,200 delegates from 160 Protestant groups met in Scotland. Called the World Missionary Conference they were the first of several ecumenical gatherings in the early and mid-twentieth century. In 1948 various of these groups got together in Amsterdam and formed the World Council of Churches.

Impact: The World Council of Churches does not make binding decisions on its members but attempts to provide consensus among member groups on issues ranging from racism and poverty to worker's rights and social justice.

Number 112: The Christian Democracy movement

In continental Europe after World War II, a new political philosophy called Christian Democracy arose. Based on the writings of such philosophers as Jacques Maritain (1882-1973) Christian Democrats used secular interpretations of certain Christian principles as the basis for promoting social equality.

Impact: Christian Democrats became the strongest political party in post-war Italy, Germany, and the Netherlands. Their strength has waned in recent decades due to their center-right political stances and corruption scandals.

Number 113: The Billy Graham Crusades begin

In 1949 Billy Graham, a Southern Baptist minister, launched his first major evangelistic crusade in Los Angeles. Prior to this he had served as an evangelist for Torrey Johnson, the founder of Youth for Christ, in small crusades around the United States and even Great Britain. It wasn't until his eight-week series of services in Los Angeles, however, that he became the most famous preacher in America. Each day the crowds grew larger as a number of popular celebrities, members of the press, and local politicians came to see what the fuss was about. He was also aided by his willingness to include all local churches in his crusade, a pattern he has continued throughout his ministry.

Impact: The list of accomplishments achieved by Billy Graham during his fruitful life is too lengthy to itemize. What can be said with certainty is that from publishing to mass media to education, he has used every tool at his disposal to spread the Gospel. The result is that an estimated 100 million people have heard him preach and over two million have made a commitment to Christ.

Number 114: Popular Christian thinkers

During the middle part of the twentieth century a number of scholarly Christians from around the world came to prominence and their works were widely received, even among nonbelievers. Included among these illustrious names are T. S. Eliot from America, J. R. R. Tolkien from England, Francois Mauriac from France, and Toyohiko Kagawa from Japan. Perhaps best known is England's C. S. Lewis. Born in Belfast, Ireland and educated at Oxford, Lewis was a professor of medieval and Renaissance literature at Cambridge. He described his conversion to Christianity from atheism in the 1955 book *Surprised by Joy*. He was a lecturer on ethical and religious matters on the BBC and wrote numerous influential books, including *Mere Christianity*, *The Screwtape Letters*, and the children's classics *The Chronicles of Narnia*.

Impact: These and other scholars influenced many people to become Christians who might not have considered the faith otherwise, especially college students.

Number 115: Protestant - Catholic Ecumenicism

In the 1920s certain Catholic and Anglican leaders got together in Belgium to seek ways that the two groups could reconcile. Pope Pius XI responded by writing that reconciliation was not possible between "true and false Christianity."

Impact: By the time of the Second Vatican Council in 1962 Pope John XXIII had taken a more conciliatory tone

by stating that Protestants and Catholics should meet
regularly to pray for unity.

Number 116: Martin Luther King and the American civil rights movement

Martin Luther King, Jr. (1929-1968) was born in Atlanta,
Georgia and studied at Morehouse College, Crozer
Theological Seminary, and Boston University. In 1954 he
became a pastor in Montgomery, Alabama at the Dexter
Avenue Baptist Church. He was later co-pastor with his
father of the Ebenezer Baptist Church in Atlanta, a church
founded by his grandfather. In Montgomery in 1955, Rosa
Parks, a respected member of the local NAACP, was
arrested after refusing to give up her seat on a bus to a
white passenger. This event followed years of mistreatment
by bus drivers who had forced black riders to sit in the
backs of buses. King was chosen to head the Montgomery
Improvement Association, which had organized a boycott
to protest the unfair practices of the bus companies. After
more than a year of peaceful protests and savage attacks
from white segregationists, the Supreme Court upheld a
previous Federal ruling and desegregated the bus lines.
King's national stature rose and in 1957 he helped found
the Southern Christian Leadership Conference (SCLC).
Jailed and threatened many times, King and his followers
worked tirelessly to end racial discrimination. Among his
many famous speeches was the "I Have a Dream" message
he gave at a massive protest in Washington, D.C. in 1963.
Here he shared his hopes for the civil rights movement

and how it would improve the lives of all Americans. His efforts earned the Nobel Peace Prize in 1964. Sadly, as he often predicted, he was assassinated in 1968 in Memphis.
Impact: King's application of the Christian principles of non-violence changed the social landscape of the United States.

Number 117: The Second Vatican Council
In 1962 Pope John XXIII called an ecumenical council in Rome a mere three months after he had been elected. Many significant changes came out of this gathering including acceptance of the mass in common languages rather than Latin, the acceptance of both clergy and laypeople in ministerial roles, and the recognition that Scripture and not tradition was the primary source of God's revelation.
Impact: While many conservative Catholics decried the decisions that came out of Vatican II, most embraced the changes and the short-term results were largely a more committed and biblically educated laity.

Number 118: The modern Pentecostal movement
While the modern Pentecostal movement actually began with the Azusa Street Revival early in the twentieth century, its growth really exploded in the 1960s. Today Pentecostalism is the largest distinctive group among Protestants and Catholics. This is just as true in Christian communities around the world as it is in North America. Pentecostal churches are growing dramatically in Africa,

Asia, Europe, and among the nations that comprised the former Soviet Union. Pentecostal church groups include the Church of God, Pentecostal Holiness churches, the Assemblies of God, and the International Church of the Foursquare Gospel.

Impact: It is estimated that over half a billion people in over a 100 nations are practicing Pentecostals.

Number 119: The growth of the Chinese church under Communism

After Mao's Cultural Revolution in 1966 it was feared that the Christian church in that coutnry would be exterminated. The oppressive policies of the Cultural Revolution remained in effect until 1976, the year Mao died. In 1979 churches were allowed to gradually reopen. Surprisingly it was discovered that during the decade of persecution the number of Chinese Christians had actually grown. This was because small, secret gatherings had taken place in homes around the country. Group fellowship had built a special bond between believers and strengthened their commitment.

Impact: It's not known exactly how many Chinese are Christian. What is certain is that opposition from the government remains to one degree or another. Yet, regardless of whether the repression is brutal or passive, Chinese believers continue to bravely live out their faith.

Number 120: The evangelical movement

The evangelical movement in the twentieth century has focused on publishing, missionary outreach, and the preservation of key conservative doctrines. These doctrines include viewing Christ and the Trinity in terms consistent with the Nicene Creed, the imminent return of Christ to gather up the faithful, and recognition of Scripture as the inerrant Word of God.

Impact: Since World War II the evangelical movement has steadily gained prominence within denominations and among believers with the establishment of educational institutions like Fuller Theological Seminary and the Institute for Worship Studies, publications like *Christianity Today* and *World Magazine*, and organizations like the National Association of Evangelicals and the Christian Booksellers Association.

Number 121: Modern Christianity in Asia

Apart from China, Christianity in Asia is growing in churches in the Philippines, Vietnam, Korea, and Taiwan. Missionaries are also active in difficult places like Tibet, Nepal, Myanmar, and Thailand.

Impact: Despite government opposition in some cases and threats from Muslims in others, Christianity is growing in nearly every Asian nation.

Number 122: Modern Christianity in Africa

Nearly half of all Africans are members of a Christian church – this despite oppression from Muslims, yearly famines, and devastating diseases like AIDS. Interestingly, despite the hurdles they face in their own countries, African Anglican bishops have begun sending oversight missionaries to the West in an effort to provide conservative leadership for disenfranchised Episcopalians who have left their denomination over the election of a gay bishop.

Impact: The growth of the African churches shows no sign of abating in the face of persecution and hardship.

Number 123: Modern Christianity in Latin America

Although Latin America is traditionally Roman Catholic, evangelical Protestant churches – especially Pentecostal groups – have grown significantly in the last 25 years.

Impact: Mission agencies continue to work in Latin American countries, providing spiritual hope and working for social justice. Evangelists like Luis Palau have witnessed tremendous acceptance for the Gospel message at revival gatherings.